Anytime, Anywhere

JOHN H. GROBERG

DESERET BOOK
SALT LAKE CITY, UTAH

Visit us at DeseretBook.com

Library of Congress Cataloging-in-Publication Data

Groberg, John H.
Anytime, anywhere / John H. Groberg.
p. cm.
Includes index.
ISBN-13: 978-1-59038-643-9 (hardbound : alk. paper)
ISBN-10: 1-59038-643-4
1. Groberg, John H. 2. Church of Jesus Christ of Latter-day Saints—Clergy—Biography. 3. Mormon Church—Clergy—Biography. 4. Missionaries—United States—Biography. 5. Missionaries—Tonga—Biography. 6. Church of Jesus Christ of Latter-day Saints—Missions. 7. Mormon Church—Missions. I. Title.
BX8695.G76A3 2006
266'.93092—dc22
[B] 2006014222

Printed in the United States of America
Worzalla Publishing Co., Stevens Point, WI

10 9 8 7 6 5 4 3 2 1

Contents

Acknowledgments

I acknowledge the faithfulness and steadiness of my wife, Jean. I love her with all my heart. Without her patience and goodness, none of this would have happened. She has typed and retyped (and re-re-retyped) this manuscript. I acknowledge and thank our children and their families, as well as my friends and co-workers who, over the years, have given so much help and encouragement, especially on this particular project.

I thank the wonderful people of the Islands and those from South America, Asia, Mexico, Central America, North America, and indeed from all over the world. They are all God's children with much to achieve and much to offer.

In a special way I wish to acknowledge and pay tribute to the missionaries and the youth of the Church. I have worked closely over many years with missionaries, youth, young single adults, their parents, and other leaders in all the places we have lived and visited. I have had marvelous and special associations with them, particularly at Brigham Young University in Provo, Hawaii, and Idaho, and at schools and institutes throughout the world.

I dedicate this book to the youth, including my own children and grandchildren, and say: You are sons and daughters of God.

You are the hope of the world. Resting on your shoulders is the future of the Church and the world. I know that with God's help you and your future families can and will live the gospel fully and carry off this saving assignment with dignity and success. Never question your heritage, your ability, or your destiny.

Always remember that God loves you, has faith in you, and will help you. Love and faith, like life and light, are not limited by time or space, but reach through the depths of eternity to touch those who are prepared to receive them. Prepare well, listen well, follow the guidance of His spirit *anytime, anywhere,* and the future is secure.

This work is an account of my own experiences. It is not an official publication of the Church. I alone am responsible for the views it expresses.

John H. Groberg

Chapter 1

ANYTIME, ANYWHERE

Shortly before general conference in April 1976, President Spencer W. Kimball telephoned me in Idaho Falls and asked if I could come to his office in Salt Lake City for a visit. I had been serving as a Regional Representative for the past seven years, and I knew that President Kimball had recently returned from the islands of the Pacific. I thought he might have some questions about the work there. Jean was used to my frequent trips to Utah for business and Church matters, so the trip seemed quite normal.

I drove to Salt Lake and went to President Kimball's office, and we visited. He expressed appreciation for my observations about the islands and for my service there. Then, with clear prophetic purpose, he called me to serve as a full-time General Authority. I was overwhelmed!

As we concluded our "visit," President Kimball asked if I had any questions. The first thing that came to my mind was: "Does this mean we will have to leave Idaho Falls?" Considering what he had just said, that was a silly question!

Rather than being upset, however, President Kimball came over and, from the depths of his magnanimous heart, reached up and gave me a big bear hug. With a twinkle in his eyes, he looked straight into my heart and tenderly said: "I know exactly how you feel. I didn't want to leave Arizona, either. It is good to love your hometown and your roots, but yes, this will mean moving anytime, anywhere in the whole world, for the rest of your life." At that moment I felt so loved by President Kimball and so certain he was a prophet that all other questions simply evaporated.

As I drove back to Idaho Falls, I reflected many times on President Kimball's words "anytime, anywhere." I thought of Peter's charge to "be ready *always* to give an answer to *every* man," and of Alma's admonition "to stand as witnesses of God at *all times* and in *all things*, and in *all places*" (1 Peter 3:15; Mosiah 18:9; emphasis added).

When I arrived home, I told Jean what had happened. We held each other tightly for a long time. Tears, questions, prayers, and assurances came naturally. We knew President Kimball was a prophet and spoke for God. We were not sure what lay ahead, but we were at peace.

I suppose one of the reasons I asked my "silly question" was that our roots were very deep in Idaho Falls. I had never anticipated leaving there. My great-grandfather and great-grandmother and my grandfather and grandmother had lived there. My parents had lived there all their married life. My father was born in Idaho Falls, and I was born and raised there, as were all ten of my brothers and sisters. Jean and I had lived in Idaho Falls all of our married life, except when we were away at school or on our mission to Tonga. We had ten children at this time, nine of whom had been born in Idaho Falls—all delivered by the same doctor, in the same hospital. Our oldest daughter was ready to graduate from Idaho Falls High School, and our youngest was starting to "get around" at nine months of age.

There were playmates close by for everyone. Often at mealtimes we would end up with one or two extra neighbor children, then call or receive calls from neighbors saying they had some of

The Groberg family in front of their home in Idaho Falls about the time of President Kimball's call to go "anytime, anywhere."

ours. After everyone was accounted for, each family fed whoever was there. We all kept track of each other. We loved our home, our neighborhood, our ward, our friends, our work, and everything about Idaho Falls. We had some big plans for our lives and were just getting in a position to carry them out. Those plans would be altered, of course, for it was God's plans, not ours, that would be carried out.

Over and over again, we reviewed President Kimball's compassionate and inspired words: "I know just how you feel . . . but yes, this will mean moving anytime, anywhere for the rest of your life." How we appreciated his empathy and his clear direction! We determined to do whatever was asked of us, without complaining or looking back. We knew in Whom we trusted and into Whose hands we were committing our lives and the lives of our family members. In a way, we were "troubled on every side," but filled with peace (see 2 Corinthians 4:8).

After being sustained and set apart, we received our first assignment: Move from Idaho Falls to Hawaii and establish the

John and Jean at the time of their call to move to Hawaii.

new Hawaii—Pacific Islands Area of the Church. This going "anytime, anywhere" was no longer theoretical—it was a reality!

Over the next thirty years, our family would move eight times to various locations throughout the world. Our children would graduate from five different high schools on four different continents. Both of our sons and four of our daughters would serve missions, and our children, together with their spouses, would speak ten different languages. Our lives were filled with challenges, opportunities, blessings, and a spectrum of experiences we never would have imagined. Through it all, we felt God's hand encouraging, protecting, guiding, and blessing us.

The experiences shared in this book are representative of the many growing and learning experiences we have had or observed during our thirty years of going anytime, anywhere the Lord has sent us. This book is not about any particular time or place, and especially not about my particular calling. My desire is that sharing these firsthand experiences may help others understand and appreciate more fully God's eternal and unlimited love for all of His children, in all places and at all times. I know that as we put forth sincere effort to love and obey God and show our appreciation for His love—whenever, wherever, and however we can—timeless and boundless blessings flow from heaven.

To me, there are no high or low callings, just different types of opportunities to overcome selfishness and learn to love and serve other people wherever we are. That is what God expects of us. President Hinckley has clearly stated: "Your obligation is as serious in your sphere of responsibility as is my obligation in my sphere. No calling in this church is small or of little consequence. All of us in the pursuit of our duty touch the lives of others. . . . You have as great an opportunity for satisfaction in the performance of your duty as I do in mine" (*Ensign*, May 1995, 71).

God didn't send us here just to be comfortable, He sent us here to grow. Growing requires effort and stretching, which usually are not comfortable. God has something important for each of us to do. For some it may require leaving lands and family without even an opportunity to "bid them farewell" (see Luke 9:57–62). Others who express a desire and willingness to travel may instead be asked to "return to thine own house, and shew how great things God hath done unto thee" (Luke 8:39). Many will be asked to leave, then return, then leave again, while others will be asked to stay put. The Lord gave Brigham Young many assignments to leave his family and go on missions to faraway places, but on at least one occasion He told him to stay home and strengthen his family and the Saints (see Doctrine and Covenants 126:1–3).

We may not understand why certain things are asked of us. At times we may even feel that we aren't up to the task. The point is, we do what the Lord wants us to do, when He wants us to do it—not what we want to do, or when we want to do it. His wisdom is infinite, ours is not. As we obey Him, over time our will and our joy will become like His.

Chapter 2

MONGOLIA

In the early 1990s the Church was getting a fledgling start in Mongolia, through many prayers and much effort by several courageous missionary couples. In 1993 Mongolia was dedicated for the preaching of the gospel by Elder Neal A. Maxwell. In 1994, as a member of the Asia Area Presidency living in Hong Kong, I was assigned responsibility for several new areas, including Mongolia. When I first visited the handful of missionaries and members there, I felt good about the progress of the work.

A few months after that visit, I received the disturbing news that a government official in Mongolia had determined to not allow any more visas for our missionaries. Shocked with this unforeseen turn of events, our Area Presidency reported it to our contact in the Quorum of the Twelve at Church headquarters. He said he would do some checking and call us back. The following day I was asked to go to Mongolia immediately and do all in my power to solve the problem.

Our daughter Jennie Marie had recently finished her mission in Slovenija and was visiting us in Hong Kong before returning to school at BYU. We quickly made arrangements for Jean, Jennie, and myself to go to Mongolia. You can imagine our heavy hearts as well as our fervent prayers as we undertook this assignment. We didn't know what had caused the problem or what direction to take when we got there. But, relying on the Lord, we flew to Mongolia to do all we could to "solve the problem."

We met with the few members we had in Ulaanbaatar and found that the situation was even more serious than we had understood. Having been under Russian Communist domination for seventy years, many government officials were still steeped in the old ways and found it difficult to change their hearts and minds.

We took some local Church leaders and met with the man who had made the decision to terminate the visas. He seemed cold and determined to stick to his decision. We met with several other government officials, some of whom were more sympathetic, but all of them said that the first official had the power to make the final decision, and there wasn't much they or we could do about it. For several days we held meetings with every official who would meet with us. We hit a dead end every time.

We decided to hold a special fast with all the members and missionaries. At the conclusion of this fast meeting, we asked if anyone had any other contacts we could consider or any new feelings about what we should do. Looking rather forlorn, they sadly shook their heads. Then one person said he had heard that a government official who had previously been friendly to the missionaries had just flown in for an emergency visit. This particular official was now assigned as an ambassador in Europe, but had returned to Mongolia to visit his son, who had been in a serious accident and was in the hospital. It was a thin thread, but we arranged to meet with him early the next morning.

We pled our cause to the ambassador, who said there was nothing he could do, as he no longer had much influence among the people who made those decisions. He informed us that his son's condition was not as serious as they had first thought, so

Jennie, John, and their official Mongolian driver.

he would be returning to Europe the next day. Almost as an afterthought, he said he had to hurry back because they had just added a new country to his ambassadorial responsibilities, and in a few days he needed to present his papers in Ljubljana, the capital of Slovenija. He had never been to Slovenija and was concerned about having time to get briefed with the right information.

I responded: "I have a daughter with me who just returned from Slovenija, where she served as a missionary. She lived in Ljubljana for eighteen months. Maybe she could answer some of your questions." He was surprised and asked if she spoke the language and knew the people, the city, and other details. I assured him she did. He was anxious to get this information, so we arranged for them to meet.

The ambassador was impressed with Jennie's understanding of Slovenija and the fact that she had been a missionary there. He was not aware that we had sister missionaries, as up to that time we had sent only elders to Mongolia. We explained our worldwide missionary activities and how they involved young men, young women, and married couples. He drank it all in, thought deeply, and asked searching questions. He expressed his gratitude for the information we had given him on Slovenija and on our extensive missionary program. When he finished, he thought for a moment, then said, "You know, there is one person I could introduce you to who just might be able to help you with your visa challenge."

He returned to his post in Europe the next day feeling much calmer because of the information he had learned about Slovenija. That same day we met with his friend, whom he had asked to help us in any way he could. That thin thread of hope began to thicken and to hold. There were many more meetings and lots of negotiations, but in the end, the visas continued to be issued and the Church continued to grow. Under the guidance of the Lord's outstretched arm, that particular problem was solved.

I have thought about the many diverse circumstances that led up to that eventual positive outcome. Think for a moment: How had a member of the Quorum of the Twelve known, nearly two years earlier, to assign Jennie to Slovenija? How did the member in Ulaanbaatar happen to hear about the accident of the ambassador's son and to know of the father's brief return? How did the visa issue come up just as Jennie arrived in Hong Kong from Slovenija? How did our contact in the Quorum of the Twelve happen to ask me to go to Mongolia immediately and help "solve the problem"?

The convergence of so many disparate factors could be termed lucky coincidence, but we know better. The Lord knows all things (see 2 Nephi 9:20) and prepares all things well. We still need to exercise strong faith and put forth great effort, but in the end we will see that all our exertions would have been of little effect without the careful planning and guidance of our loving and infinitely knowledgeable Creator!

About a year after this event, the Mongolia Mission was formally organized. Now, about ten years later, we have a district in Ulaanbaatar and one in Darkhan, and over 5,000 members of the Church in Mongolia. Many missionaries, both Mongolian and of other nationalities, have served and continue to serve wonderful missions there, and the lives of many continue to be blessed. I hope those who have worked so hard in Mongolia will share in the joy I have felt as I vicariously represented them in "solving" this and other issues that have allowed the work of the Lord to roll forward.

I have learned that if we trust the Lord and move forward in faith, anytime, anywhere, to simply do whatever the Lord wants done, He orchestrates events so amazingly and with such miraculous efficiency that it all but takes our breath away.

Chapter 3

DARKHAN

As Jean and I boarded the train on a bitterly cold February night to travel from Ulaanbaatar to Erdenet, Mongolia, my thoughts were mostly about trying to get some rest. The "sleeper" car was rustic and run-down but still the most comfortable place on the train because at least it was somewhat heated. I tried to rest, but my mind began to wander. I thought of where I was and how at this very moment I was nearing the Russian Siberian border on my way to help carry the light of the gospel to another corner of the world.

We rattled through the night, slept fitfully, and arrived early the next morning in Erdenet, where four enthusiastic, smiling missionaries met us. We went directly to a large building where we held a meeting with the missionaries, some members, and several investigators. After the meeting we visited the schools where the four elders taught English. The school officials gave glowing reports of the good work the missionaries were doing.

We felt a spirit of love and cooperation in Erdenet and would have liked to stay longer. However, because of meetings we had scheduled the next day with the members and missionaries in Ulaanbaatar, we had to catch the return train late that same afternoon. I was not looking forward to another restless, all-night train ride, so we waited until the last possible moment to board the train. It was cold and dark when we started the long return trip to Ulaanbaatar. There is precious little to see from a frosted train window in midwinter in the center of Mongolia. I wasn't exactly enjoying the journey.

We rolled along through the night, going fast in level or downhill areas, but barely crawling up inclines. The train jerked and stopped at various small towns and seemingly obscure locations to let people off and on. I slept some, but mostly I thought about where we were and what we were doing. I reflected on my great admiration for the missionaries and the Mongolian converts who had responded to the gospel message. The Church had been established there for only three years, and already several Mongolian youth were serving missions abroad. I was filled with deep awe as I marveled at how the Lord had opened the way for the spread of His gospel of peace to a people who through much of their history had been steeped in warfare. At one time, in their fierceness and military prowess (remember Genghis Khan?), they controlled one of the largest empires in the world, stretching from China to Central Europe.

I was finally starting to drift off to sleep when suddenly I felt some extra hard jerks and found myself wide awake. I had an impression to clear a spot in the frosted window and look out. I saw a single light suspended from a small wooden pole about ten feet high. I could see no town or other lights. The train stopped, and as I looked through the frosted window I witnessed a scene I shall never forget. There in the trackless steppes of central Mongolia, huddled together under that single dim light, was a family, waiting for someone to join them from the train.

Despite the cold and darkness of the night, there were smiles of excitement and anticipation on the faces of those seven waiting people. They stood close together, bracing against the chill wind, their features clearly outlined by the light. The night sky was so dark that all I could see beyond the small cylinder of light cast by the lonely bulb was the blur of frosty snow being driven, at near-horizontal angles, to the never-ending tundra beyond.

I focused on the happy family. Each person was wearing Cossack-like boots, a heavy fur cap, and a beautifully colored, felt-lined tunic to help shield them from the cold.

I marveled at the power of that loyal lightbulb as it faithfully dispelled the darkness within its sphere of influence. It not only highlighted the smiles of that happy family but also marked the place where a weary traveler could descend from a long ride and be embraced by loved ones.

Suddenly they appeared. Not one, but three people, dressed heavily against the cold and wind, stepped down from the train. As they ran to the waiting group, I witnessed again the universal outpouring of joy that occurs when loved ones are reunited after a period of absence. The deeply touching scene was made even more memorable by the wind and cold and dark, which, though tangible, were largely dispelled by the joy of that happy family reunion. Willing hands anxiously relieved the travelers of their suitcases and boxes. For the first time I noticed an old cart and a faithful horse waiting patiently in the background. My mind and soul tried to capture the joy of being reunited—the joy of a safe journey—the joy of patient waiting rewarded—the joy of a family being together again. All of that, and more, shone brilliantly above the bleak and dreary windscape of that snow-filled night.

Soon the family moved beyond the fringes of the light, and the train slowly began to pull away. I strained to see them a little longer. I felt the brave lightbulb putting forth extra effort trying to extend its influence a little farther, just for me. Soon, however, the family was beyond my sight. As quietly as they had appeared, they disappeared into the night.

In my mind I could still see their smiles, sense their love, and feel their joy in being reunited. My heart cried out: "There they go—here I am. I must do something to help them. I have the gospel of Jesus Christ, and the charge to take it to all the world. Here I am in the heart of Mongolia in the middle of the night, amidst the dark and cold of a Siberian winter. Yet there is a family out there, a family that feels love and warmth and unity. They have the right to be together forever. I must help them. I must do something. But what? And how?"

So indelibly was that supernal scene impressed on my soul that I no longer thought of sleep. I got up and wandered down the narrow aisle. I wanted to know where we were, but was having difficulty finding anyone I could communicate with. Finally one attendant seemed to understand and pointed to a map. His finger was next to a city: Darkhan. Ah, so that was where we were—just outside of Darkhan. *Darkhan—that's it,* I thought. I became very excited. I knew I had been able to witness this family reunion for a reason. I knew we must send missionaries to Darkhan and start the work there. I was sure that was what the Lord wanted.

The rest of the night evaporated quickly. The next day, after our meetings with the missionaries in Ulaanbaatar, I asked the mission president if we could send some missionaries to Darkhan. "Oh," he said in a resigned tone, "we have tried many times. Darkhan is one of the larger cities in Mongolia, but the officials there are very much against our church. As you know, the only way we can send missionaries to Darkhan or any city in Mongolia is if the officials invite them to teach English in their schools. I have tried again and again, but they will not invite them."

"Could you try once more?" I asked.

"I called just a few weeks ago. However, if you wish, I will try again next month."

"How about calling right now?" I urged. "I have a special feeling about Darkhan."

"Right now? It has been only a few weeks since I last tried. It might irritate them."

"Would you please try right now?"

"Well, all right, if you say so," agreed the mission president.

The call was made and, sure enough, one of the schools in Darkhan had just lost two Swedish volunteer teachers who had unexpectedly needed to return to Sweden because of health problems. The officials desperately needed replacements and asked, "Could you have two of your young men here next Monday? We'll arrange a place for them to live."

The next Monday two missionaries were in Darkhan. The members in Ulaanbaatar were aware of eight members, originally from Darkhan, who had come to Ulaanbaatar and joined the Church there. Five of them had recently returned to Darkhan, so the missionaries had a starting point. As with most new areas, starting out proved to be difficult. The next several months were times of trouble and trial. But through the diligent work of the missionaries and members, and the faithful guidance of the mission president, slowly and surely the gospel took root in Darkhan.

Nearly a year after that first February train ride I called the new mission president in Ulaanbaatar and asked how things were going in Darkhan. He had arrived the previous July and was unaware of my original feelings on starting the work in that area.

"Strange you would ask," he responded. "We have just returned from Darkhan. There were fifty-two people at sacrament meeting. We are sending two more missionaries. Elder Groberg, I have had many spiritual experiences in my life as bishop, high councilor, stake president, and mission president, but I want you to know that attending sacrament meeting last Sunday in Darkhan was one of the most powerful spiritual experiences I have ever had. Two older men—both priests, both converts of just a few months—gave the sacrament prayers on the bread and the water. They gave them in Mongolian, which I did not understand, but I understood perfectly what they were doing. They literally blessed the sacrament to the souls of all those who partook of it. So powerful were those blessings that there was hardly a dry eye in the congregation. It caused me to wonder about some of the other sacrament meetings I have attended. Anyway, to answer your question, the branch in Darkhan is doing wondrously well."

As I hung up the phone, I began to relive that cold night train ride of a year earlier. In my mind I heard again the train slowly whoosh to a stop and watched a beautifully dressed, smiling family, patiently waiting, then joyfully running to meet their loved ones. I witnessed again that colorful, united family disappear into the night and felt the train slowly pull away on its way to Ulaanbaatar. I saw again that brave light straining to spread its goodness as far as it could, acting as a beacon for me to see and know that the time was right to send the true light of Christ to these wonderful people. Again I heard my heart cry out, "There they go—here I am. I must do something to help them." I remembered the conversation with the first mission president and the events that followed. Hearing the current report from the new mission president put me in a state of deep contemplation and wonder. I thanked God for His never-ending mercy, His unfailing help, and His constant love.

I do not know who the family was that unknowingly let me join in their happy reunion under the glow of a small light globe. I do not know who those people were who descended from the train into that cold, dark night in central Mongolia. I do not know whose arms encircled each other in loving hugs of joy. I do not know whose hands reached happily for suitcases and boxes and took them to a waiting horse-drawn cart. No, I do not know who those people were who so quietly, yet joyfully, disappeared into the vastness of a snowy Siberian night those many months ago.

I do not know their names and may never see their faces again, but I do know this: Some of them or some of their descendants either are or soon will be members of The Church of Jesus Christ of Latter-day Saints and belong to the kingdom of God on earth. There they will learn and understand how to be a family together forever. Such is the power of the light and the promise that is, to me, the miracle of Darkhan!

Chapter 4

DARKHAN REVISITED

From the first day the missionaries arrived in Darkhan they found some opposition but also many people anxious for the gospel. Two and a half years after our original all-night train ride, Jean and I were again assigned to visit the missionaries in Mongolia. This time we made the trip not on a cold, dark night but on a beautiful summer afternoon. When we arrived, we were met by the missionaries and several local leaders from a thriving branch. The members and missionaries were enthusiastic and full of the Spirit. I asked the branch president how many members they had. He replied that they had around 100. I asked him how many came to sacrament meeting. He seemed a little puzzled, but replied, "Around 100, of course." The mission president confirmed that the Darkhan Branch was one of the strongest branches in Mongolia, with a wonderful priesthood base.

That evening we held a meeting with the members. The branch president conducted and was the first speaker. I felt a thrill of excitement as I watched him and felt his wonderful spirit. I noticed a woman on the front row smiling with such sincerity and encouragement that I felt sure she was the branch president's wife. Something about her smile seemed familiar. The mission president confirmed that she was indeed the branch president's wife and that her father, who was in attendance, was also a member. I felt impressed to call on him to bear his testimony.

When his name was announced, an older gentleman stood and quietly came to the stand. I saw assurance in his eyes, pride in his daughter's eyes, and confidence in his son-in-law's eyes. I noticed his boots, his dress, his gait. Those smiles, that warmth, and that feeling of goodness all seemed hauntingly familiar. I knew I had seen and felt them somewhere before. As my heart and mind absorbed that scene, something moved inside me and I could hardly breathe: Could it be?

The father began his testimony: "I know The Church of Jesus Christ of Latter-day Saints is true. It is God's kingdom on earth. Every Mongolian should be a member. We must do all we can to help this happen. We should start with our families. I have eleven children—all married. Five of them and their families are now members. I am working with the other six. I don't want to die until they are all members. I want our family to be together in the Church now and forever."

He went on, but I didn't hear much more. My mind was back aboard a winter train looking through a frosted window as a family was happily reunited on a cold, dark night. I felt again those words: "There they go—here I am. I must do something to help them."

My heart throbbed. Could this be that family? I was not sure, but I *was* sure that this family from the Darkhan Branch was excited about the gospel. I knew they wanted to become an eternal family and help others do likewise. I knew they were serving as instruments in God's hand to shine forth and build His kingdom in Mongolia. That was all I needed to know. Through misty eyes I thanked the Lord for His profound love in fulfilling promises and simply said, "It is enough."

A Mongolian branch president and his family.

We are all instruments in the Lord's hands. This is His work, and He brings about His purposes using us and our light to the degree we are willing. He has set His hand once again to recover His people Israel through His gospel, from wherever they are. I am positive of that. How important it is for all of us to be faithful and obedient helpers in this ongoing saga of the gathering of Israel and the rolling forth of the kingdom of God! It truly is the most important work in all the world, and our active, anxious participation, especially in our families, is our most important task. I know we all fall short of what we want to do and be, but we can always keep trying. How wonderful to feel God's unconditional love as He constantly forgives and encourages and helps us.

Sometimes we may be jolted awake and find ourselves in a dark, cold place, as on a train in central Mongolia. But if we follow the promptings of the Spirit and look through the window of faith (even though misty), we can see the happiness and joy available for us and others. If we heed the promptings of the Spirit and take the needed action, the fulfillment of those impressions will surely come. It may take years, but as surely as I sat in that special meeting in Darkhan and literally saw the fulfillment of earlier impressions, so surely may all of us move from the cold and dark of a seemingly bleak plain of moaning wind and flying snow to a summer of light and beauty and fulfillment. Our joy can be even more real than the initial vision.

Before leaving Darkhan and continuing our visit to other parts of Mongolia, we located a piece of land for a chapel. It has moved from a plan to a physical reality, just as the testimonies of those members in Darkhan have moved from an impression to a beautiful fulfillment.

After completing our tour of Mongolia we boarded a plane for China and Hong Kong. On the same plane were five missionaries. One was an American returning to the United States, having completed his mission in Mongolia. The other four were Mongolians leaving for the Missionary Training Center in Provo, Utah, before starting their missions in California. One of the Mongolians was from Ulaanbaatar, another from Erdenet, and guess where the other two were from? That's right: Darkhan!

The miracle of Darkhan, like the miracle of each of our lives, goes on and on and on forever. Our lives are filled with beauty and potential, which we now see only as "through a glass, darkly" (1 Corinthians 13:12). We and our families can and eventually will "shine forth in the kingdom of God" (Alma 40:25) and increase in wonder and joy and beauty as we respond to the promptings of God's spirit.

I pray we will listen more carefully, obey more willingly, work more diligently, and shine more brilliantly in doing the things that are of eternal importance, and not get diverted by things of mere temporal duration. I hope we will always be prepared anytime, anywhere, to heed the whisperings of God's spirit. I know great joy always follows!

Chapter 5

THE GOBI

The missionaries in Mongolia worked mainly in the larger towns. Although they worked with everyone, they quickly found that the people who had recently moved into these towns from the outlying areas, especially those from the Gobi desert, tended to be the most receptive to the gospel. We all wondered why.

We had been told many times that we could not really understand Mongolia until we had spent time in the Gobi. Jean and I had a feeling that this was true, so we made arrangements to spend a few days in the Gobi. The only way to do that at the time was to hire a professional guide and stay in a tourist camp.

Our time in the Gobi began with an early-morning flight of about two hours, in an ancient Russian turbo-prop, from Ulaanbaatar to Juulchin. We flew over miles and miles of what appeared to be barren wasteland. Yet here and there I could see a round white *ger* (Mongolian tent home) and an occasional herd of sheep, horses, or goats. The landscape was stark but captivating. The pilot knew the area well and skillfully flew over miles of trackless terrain before descending to the desert floor.

Our landing kicked up clouds of dust that literally encased us as though we were caught in a thick desert storm. The pilot, however, knew where to go, and when the dust more or less settled we found ourselves close to our camp.

As we stepped off the little plane onto the arid Gobi soil and breathed the hot, dry air, we felt like we were walking into a gigantic baker's oven. Our guide, Bolor, a lovely young Mongolian girl who spoke excellent English as well as Russian and Mongolian, took us to our *ger.* Those original "mobile homes" are literally rolled up and transported by their nomadic owners whenever their animals need to be moved to new grazing land.

The Gobi is one of the largest deserts in the world, stretching nearly 3,000 miles across much of Southern Mongolia and Northern China. It is vast. It is beautiful. It is hot during the day, cold at night, filled with oases and life for those who know their way, but barren and unforgiving for those who do not. What was it about this area that produced such sterling qualities in its people?

That evening at camp, a desert lightning storm lit up the horizon with powerful displays of vivid, dancing light. The sky overhead, however, was perfectly clear and filled with endless constellations and sensational shooting stars. What grandeur! It was easy to see how the desert dwellers could feel the power God has and controls. The stars and the demonstration of power were like those I had experienced on the open seas in Tonga.

The next day we traveled to see the Gobi landscape and the delightful people who are the most important part of the surroundings. Our "captain" seemed to drive anywhere he pleased. You could feel the freedom in his demeanor as he navigated uninhibited by roads or other vehicles. He was "sailing" through his Gobi.

This brought back the same emotions I had felt while sailing among small islands in Tonga. When I set forth on His mighty sea in small, frail boats (but with an experienced captain) in Tonga, I always had a feeling of total dependence on God. Cruising the

John on horseback in the Gobi.

endless steppes of the Gobi in a bouncing Russian jeep (but with an experienced Mongolian driver) caused me to feel the same way. Both the endless desert and the boundless sea give me feelings of vastness, of unlimited vistas, endless expanses, and closeness to God. I was beginning to understand why the Gobi people took so well to the gospel.

We stopped at what appeared to be a vacant *ger.* However, people appeared from nowhere and invited us in for dried goat cheese, fermented mare's milk, and cultured camel's milk. We tried a tiny bit of the hard goat cheese, and that was enough. While we were there, a boy came riding up on his pony. We wondered what he was doing out alone. Our guide asked him how old he was. He nearly broke into tears as he answered, "I'm twelve years old and I've lost my camels!" "How many camels have you lost?" asked Bolor. "Five. I have to find them." "What will happen if you can't find them?" Holding back his tears, he replied, "Then I will go home and my mother will have to find them." He was really concerned about this last alternative.

Instantly our guide, our driver, and the family in the *ger* got together with the young boy and worked out a plan to find his camels. It never occurred to them to say, "Sorry, we are busy," or "Good luck." Rather, they just went to work and found his camels. Even though we were "set aside" for a while, I was immensely impressed with this automatic show of concern and help for someone in need. I was beginning to see how these people had developed the qualities that made them so special.

As we returned to camp, our guide explained that no one in the Gobi ever locks their *ger.* If they have to go off to move animals, or for some other purpose, they leave their *ger* open with food and drink available for anyone who might come by. They look out for and depend upon one another for survival. She told us that during the winter the Gobi people eat nothing but meat, and during the summer they eat mostly milk products. Still, they are healthy and strong, with beautiful, straight, white teeth. As we saw occasional herds of camels or horses eating where there seemed to be nothing to eat, it caused me to realize how a loving Father has put within the reach of all His children that which they need to survive and even thrive. I sensed His love for these Gobi people and how pleased He is with their desire to help one another.

That night we stayed up late taking time-exposure photos of the brilliant stars. We were so far north that it was still light in the western sky at 11:00 P.M. I walked that night in the desert. Whenever a breeze came up I stopped, closed my eyes, stretched out my arms, and felt myself once more on a small sailboat gliding through the waters of the Pacific or even through the endless spaces of eternity. The feelings were deep, profound, and real. I sensed again how people in these environments are drawn closer to God.

As I reflected on the instinctive desire the Gobi people have to help one another, my mind went back to Tonga. I thought of the countless voyages I had taken in small sailboats and remembered how often the captain would suddenly change course. When I asked him why, he would respond that he thought he saw something that might be another boat or person in need. Most of the time what he saw would turn out to be some drifting log or other flotsam, but he always turned to make sure. Can you imagine the feelings when occasionally there *was* a boat in distress!

I am certain that one of the reasons the Tongans and the Mongolians embrace the gospel so readily has to do with their environment and their desire and need to help one another. On the surface of a vast "ocean"—whether of water or sand—they cannot help but feel insignificant when compared to God's greatness. They know they need help from a higher power just to survive. Should we not all feel the same as we cruise through space on this small planet earth? The people of the Gobi are raised with a built-in desire to work hard and to look after each other.

I thought of the stark contrast this is to our living in high-rise apartments or spacious mansions, where the rush and bustle of man and his toys crowds out thoughts of God. Too often, the bright city lights obscure or even eliminate our view of the stars and the endless heavens beyond. Little wonder that people living closer to nature tend to be more worshipful of a Divine Creator, while those living surrounded by the creations of man find it more difficult.

The next morning we drove in yet another direction, where we visited other Mongolians, entered their *gers*, rode their camels, and drank their camel's milk (it tastes something like strange yogurt). The people of the Gobi are sincerely friendly. I was impressed that everyone—from the youngest child to the oldest grandparent—was busy with some important responsibility. At

A Mongolian family in a traditional ger.

one *ger* we got a referral of a young Mongolian student who would be attending a school in Ulaanbaatar, where two of our missionaries were teaching English. The family was excited for their son to meet the missionaries. Our guide also agreed to see the missionaries when she returned to Ulaanbaatar.

When our prearranged time came to a close, we were reluctant to leave the hauntingly beautiful Gobi desert. We now saw the Mongolian members with different eyes as we understood their background and heritage a little better. When we see people as they really are and picture them as they can become, it makes everything we do more effective. The Gobi had changed our perspective in more ways than one.

On our way back to Ulaanbaatar we met with the missionaries stationed in one of the towns on the edge of the desert where many of the Gobi people come for supplies and mail. They were full of enthusiasm. They knew as we now did that these people make good members largely because their very nature is to help one another. They do not see other people as competitors, enemies, or even potential customers, but as fellow travelers on this planet—at times in need of help, at other times as those who can give needed help. We all need to be more instinctive about sensing the needs of others and assisting them more readily.

There are more people lost and wounded in the "desert places" of life or struggling in the torrential waves of the sea of sin than we can now imagine. We need to find them before they drown or perish from thirst and guide them to the Living Water and the Bread of Life that the Savior supplies. Maybe only when our desire to help becomes the very essence of our character will we be truly ready not only to sail the open seas or roam the endless deserts, but to move with confidence through the universe.

On our flight from Ulaanbaatar to Beijing there were four Mongolian missionaries on their way to the Missionary Training Center in Provo. None of them had been out of Mongolia before, and only one had ever been on a plane. I helped them find their seats and buckle their seat belts. There were tears in their eyes as we took off from Mongolia. I observed them cramped in small seats, strapped down with unfamiliar restraints, listening to strange words, surrounded by strange people in a small, confined space. I thought back to the Gobi—of the freedom of horses and camels, of space and distance, of *gers* filled with food and drink, of families willing and anxious to help anyone—and my throat choked with emotion for them. They were leaving all of this to preach the gospel to people in Utah and California. Willing to be confined for a while, they will pass through the vortex of faith and obedience and find themselves freer than they could ever imagine. What faith—what courage!

As we continued on to Hong Kong, I closed my eyes and reflected on our experience in the Gobi. I thought of the Mongolians who automatically helped a young boy find his lost camels in a vast desert, then of a Tongan sea captain who quickly changed his course when he sensed the possibility of someone in need, then of a good Samaritan quietly stopping to help a wounded traveler. I wondered if he was from a desert place like the Gobi. I remembered how much the Savior extolled these virtues and hoped I could do better. I thought of Moses spending forty years in the desert as a shepherd before returning to Egypt to fulfill his mission. I wondered if the desert camps and oases in Moses' day were as open and welcoming to those in need as the *gers* in the Gobi are today.

How I hope we can learn from the people of the Gobi and keep our hearts and minds open and welcoming to those in need. As we spend time, either actually or in our hearts, in places like deserts and oceans and mountains, we will naturally feel more inclined to welcome and help those in need of food, drink, or shelter, whether physical or spiritual. I know that as we love and serve others with all our hearts, the day will come when our desire and ability to help those in need will be as boundless as the seas and as endless as the sands of the Gobi.

Chapter 6

BEATING RETREAT

When I was serving in the Asia Area Presidency, Jean and I traveled occasionally to India. One such visit occurred when the Indians were celebrating the fiftieth anniversary of their country's independence from Great Britain. Our friends from the Indian government and the American Embassy told us that the annual "Beating Retreat" ceremony was an event not to be missed, especially in this jubilee year. They made arrangements for us to attend, sitting in a reserved section of the huge parade area between government buildings where the ceremony would be held.

Exactly one hour before sundown, the fanfare started. The Camel Corps moved into position atop the inside walls of the massive government buildings on each side of the entrance to the public square. The camels, bedecked with fancy saddles and tasseled bridles, proudly bore riders holding rifles in front of them in a vertical salute. Silhouetted against the setting sun, they stood at attention, acting as silent sentinels guarding this special presentation.

From a distance the combined Army, Navy, and Air Force Bands, of several hundred each, struck up "Semper Fidelis" and marched from the buildings into the great parade ground and toward the thousands of spectators. Their uniforms were spectacular. The beautiful turbans, hats, white chaps, black boots, braids, frills, guns, and uniforms of the Army (brown), Navy (blue), and Air Force (grey) were as neat and crisp as you could see anywhere. The quality of the music, the exactness of their marching, the splendor of their uniforms, and the colorfulness of their varied headgear was truly a once-in-a-lifetime experience.

Next came the precision horse riding unit. It was almost like an equestrian ballet as the horses bowed and pranced this way and that in perfect unison, while the bugles blared in thrilling cadence.

They were followed by the Indian Bagpipe Corps. What a mournful yet captivating sound they made as they maneuvered through well-choreographed formations that seemed endlessly original. Then the Gurkha Bugle Corps came to the front. The Gurkhas were the only group in India and Nepal that the British never could defeat. The British finally hired them to fight as mercenaries for Britain, which they have done with distinction for around 200 years.

John and Jean in India.

After them came the Drum Corps, some of whom wore full tiger skins—heads, tails, and all. They were amazing with their coordinated pounding and twirling and clicking of drumsticks. The roll of drums from soft to loud, left to right, and front to back, like rolls of thunder echoing across a great valley, was so well done that it held us spellbound.

All of these groups now assembled in the square, and a richly dressed conductor walked to the podium and led the entire group in a beautiful rendition of Brahms' "Lullaby." It was in such stark contrast to the previous loud martial music that the whole audience practically fell into a swoon. Then, to make things even more beautiful, the bands softened to a whisper, and from a distant tower turret on the left came the clear, penetrating sound of a single trumpet through the crisp air. Heads turned and eyes strained to focus on where the beautiful sound was coming from. The solo trumpet and the band then crescendoed in perfect unison and repeated that beautiful melody. "How could anything be lovelier?" I thought. Once again the band softened to a whisper, and from a tower on the right another solo trumpet, as rich and mellow as the first, rendered its matching musical message of peace. The band again swelled in support of the two solo trumpets. As the final "lullaby and good night" faded into the distance, a soft, echolike repeat floated across the assembly from yet a third distant tower in the opposite direction. We were totally caught up in the pervasive beauty of the sights, sounds, pageantry, and nostalgia of an India from a day gone by.

After the various groups did some more marching, drumming, energetic playing and changing of positions, another conductor came to the podium. Now the combined military bands became as a beautiful organ. They played the hauntingly beautiful theme from Dvorak's *New World Symphony* commonly known as "Going Home." When we thought nothing could possibly be more moving, the combined bands softened their sound, and the beautiful melody "Going Home, Going Home" resonated from chimes set high in distant turrets.

As this nostalgic melody came to a close, all the bands again marched and twirled and played martial music until just a few minutes before sundown. Then, with everyone at full attention, the national anthem was played. At a special cue, everything stopped, and a bedazzling color guard came forward to retire the colors. You could feel that the hearts of the Indians present were swollen in pride. As the Indian flag was slowly lowered from its mast at the far end of the parade ground, we assumed that was the end of this spectacular evening.

But no, there was yet one more offering. When the flag reached half-mast, the band, the horses, and everyone quieted to an almost other-worldly silence. A new conductor came to the podium, and with the wave of his baton one of the most beautiful renditions of "Abide with Me" I have ever heard filled the air. The Indians knew that this was Mahatma Gandhi's favorite piece of music. It was the only one he requested be played at his funeral.

Amidst the pageantry and splendor of modern-day India, the little man of peace was remembered again. The slow lowering of the Indian flag kept perfect cadence with this beloved hymn. When the flag was taken from the mast and reverently folded, distant echoes of "Abide with Me" from all directions filled the entire assembly with wonder and feelings of goodness.

It was surely over now. Just as the last fold of the flag was made, the sun set, and immediately thousands of lights burst on, outlining all the major government buildings. When everyone had caught their breath, a spontaneous and tremendous round of applause filled the area. I looked around and saw faces filled with pride and eyes filled with tears. It was an extremely moving experience for Indians and foreigners alike.

We stood quietly as the Camel Corps rode into the distance and the horses, bands, drums, and bagpipes all moved down a

Typical scene of Indian children carrying water pots on their heads.

long, wide promenade and finally disappeared. The "Retreat" had been "Beaten." The British were gone, but the Indians who were now in charge still showed respect for the legacy left, not only by the British, but more movingly by a little old man, often dressed only in a loincloth, who for years walked the Indian countryside, speaking of peace and unity among a disparate populace. This night he moved again among his beloved people, encouraging them to be soft and kind, to love one another, and to plead to God, however they pictured Him, to "abide with them."

We will always have a better feeling toward India because of this experience. As in other countries, there are still serious problems and much hard work to do; there is treachery, poverty, misrepresentation, arrogance, evil, sickness, even slavery of sorts. But there is also hope, for the Indian people continue to revere a wise man who said war and killing and revenge were not the right way, but nonviolence and unity and character were the keys to lasting peace.

Truly, the blessings of the Lord are to be found anytime, anywhere in the world where people strive for good!

Chapter 7

Take No Thought

Something unusual began to happen about fifty years after my first mission to Tonga. More and more Tongans began inviting Jean and me, and often members of our family, to various events. I felt a strong desire to accept as many of these invitations as possible. The Tongan Saints love to share experiences, express appreciation, and show their love in the ways they know best—singing, dancing, feasting, and offering formal poetic oratory. During this period Jean and I and others were blessed in many ways as we attended dozens of these celebrations.

Many of the people who invited us were reaching their final years in mortality and wanted to tell experiences and express feelings with their extended families present. In most cases the stories they shared were about something I had barely been aware of at the time and had essentially forgotten. I sensed they recognized that fact and sincerely desired to bring those memories back. It worked. Once they began talking about happenings some fifty years ago, long-dormant memories were awakened and came flooding into my mind as though they had just happened.

During my first mission, it was difficult to find people willing to listen because of the pervasive antagonism or at least dismissive attitude toward the Church. I pled with the Lord to help me with the language and give me love for and understanding of the Tongan people, and to show me how to effectively impart the gospel to them. The impression I received was to keep trying and to continue studying the language and the scriptures, especially the Old Testament. Even with better language ability, scriptural understanding, and careful planning, I was still rebuffed so many times that I became disheartened. Why would anyone—especially these descendants of Joseph—not want the blessings of the gospel? All my study and planning seemed for naught. I couldn't figure it out.

Not knowing what else to do, I continued studying, praying, and working hard. Over time the impression came to me that I should just go out among the people each day and take no thought beforehand of where I would go or what I would say, but rely on the Spirit to guide me. As I followed those promptings, opportunities to teach and testify came about in ways I would never have dreamed. It was a literal fulfillment of the Lord's promise: "Neither take ye thought beforehand what ye shall say; but treasure up in your minds continually the words of life, and it shall be given you in the very hour that portion that shall be meted unto every man" (Doctrine and Covenants 84:85).

Many of the experiences that ultimately meant so much to those involved had not made a particularly strong impact on me at the time. But by attending these special events many decades later, I was blessed to learn how the Lord through His tender mercies brought about many miracles. In retrospect I can see how surely He kept His promise: "Therefore, verily I say unto you, lift up your voices unto this people; speak the thoughts that I shall put into your hearts, and you shall not be confounded before men; For it shall be given you in the very hour, yea, in the very moment, what ye shall say. . . . [And] the Holy Ghost shall be shed forth in bearing record unto all things whatsoever ye shall say" (Doctrine and Covenants 100:5–8).

Following are a few of the stories told to me at those events, all of which illustrate God's active goodness among a people of faith.

THE MARRIAGE

A Tongan couple reminded me that fifty years ago, as a young missionary, I had performed their marriage. (Missionaries were authorized to perform marriages back then, and I officiated at many of them.) They told me about their large family of descendants, many of whom served as missionaries and married in the temple. When I thanked them for their efforts, they became emotional and said, "No, we thank you." The husband continued, "I was an inactive deacon at the time you married us, but something you said during the marriage ceremony struck me profoundly. It gave me a desire to become active in the Church and raise our family according to what you said."

I must have looked rather blank, for although I remembered performing their marriage, I could not remember exactly what I

A traditional Tongan marriage group.

had said. They both responded immediately, "Don't you remember when you told us what a great blessing it was to have one Israelite marry another Israelite? You said that as pure descendants of Abraham, Isaac, and Jacob, we not only were entitled to receive great blessings but had a solemn responsibility to have a family and raise a righteous posterity. This way our children, as pure Israelites, could marry other Israelites and help fulfill the promise made to Abraham, that in his seed the whole world would be blessed. This became our family goal, and we have done our best to fulfill it. We have since been sealed in the temple and we know what you said and what we have done is according to God's will. Thank you for starting us off in the right direction."

It was amazing and humbling to me to realize that the Lord put into the mind and mouth of a young missionary the exact words from the Old Testament needed to launch this family into their eternal potential. As I looked at them with deep love, I recognized that although their bodies were older, their spirits still sparkled. I thanked them again for their faithfulness, and we parted.

When I returned home, I looked in my journal of fifty years earlier and found this brief entry: "*Today I performed the marriage of Sione and Mele. They are good kids and will do well.*" Nothing more. The true record of that event resides in the hearts and souls of this fine couple and their family. They took the spiritually prompted words that had been humbly and purely planted fifty years ago, and with faith and obedience allowed the Lord to bring about their fulfillment.

THE SICK BOY

A Tongan family asked us to come to a special get-together. They had lived in Hawaii for many years but had flown to Salt Lake City for this occasion so they could express their gratitude. When we arrived at the home we found an elaborate feast

Students at the Church-sponsored Deseret School in Ha'apai, Tonga.

prepared, with many family members and friends present. After the sumptuous meal, an older woman stood and spoke. She explained that her husband was deaf and could not speak, so she would represent him. (*Kolipoki* was the Tongans' name for me.)

"Kolipoki, you remember how opposed I was to you and to the Church. I wanted nothing to do with it, and every time I saw you coming, I ran away. I saw to it that my husband did not participate even though he was a member of record. You finally convinced me that because of my husband's membership I should at least let our children come to your school and also attend Primary. Since Primary was held on Tuesday afternoon, I agreed. We all went to my church on Sunday.

"Then one day, our oldest son, who was seven, became very ill. He was taken to the hospital and his condition went steadily downhill. You asked about giving him a blessing, and I refused. After many days the doctor told me there was nothing more they could do, and since there was no hope for him, I was told I must take him home the next day and let him die there. That evening I had a dream in which I saw the face of the branch Primary president. She smiled so beautifully at me that I knew I must speak to her.

"Early the next morning I found her and told her of my dream. She said I should ask Kolipoki to give my son a blessing. I was embarrassed, as I remembered how I had scorned you in the past. But I told her that if she would ask Kolipoki to give my son a blessing, I would not interfere.

"When the Primary president talked to you, you went straight to the hospital and asked for me. I tried to hide, but you found me. You asked if I had faith in the Lord Jesus Christ. I said I did. I was glad you didn't ask if I had faith in you or your church. Then, even though I turned away and left the room, you still gave my son a blessing. After you finished, I tiptoed back and saw you kneeling in prayer and heard you say: 'Father in Heaven, please help the mother of this young boy to have sufficient faith that he might be healed. I know Thou canst do this. She is a good woman. It will require a miracle to heal the boy, but an even greater miracle to heal his mother's heart. Please do both. In the name of Jesus Christ, Amen.'

"I turned away, racked with sorrow and filled with tears. I thought I saw a light encircling you and my son as you prayed. I asked God to please forgive me and give me faith. I watched you leave the hospital as evening descended and I could still see that glow. I was too embarrassed to say anything to you, but for the first time I felt love for you, faith in you, and faith in the Lord and in the blessing you had given.

"The next moment I heard the doctor saying, 'It is evening, time to take your boy home. Come, I'll help you.'

"We went to his room. He was sitting up in bed, and for the first time in weeks, he spoke clearly. He asked if he could get dressed and go home. I was amazed, as was the doctor who knew Kolipoki had been there a short time ago. He looked at me and simply said, 'There is a greater doctor above. You won't need my help to take your son home.'

"My son got dressed, and we walked home. As soon as we got home, I sent for you. When you came, you embraced me and my son and asked if we could have a prayer—which we did. It was a beautiful prayer. I remember how you thanked God for healing my son, but especially thanked Him for softening my heart and giving me faith. As soon as the prayer was finished, I told you I wanted to be baptized. You said that would be fine, but you needed to explain what would be expected of me as a member. I invited some of my friends to come, and we spent several days being instructed by you. That weekend you baptized me and four of my friends. Shortly thereafter you finished your mission and returned to America.

"I'm here today to tell you how much all of this has meant to me, my husband, and our family. All of our sons have served missions, and the son who was miraculously healed now has two sons of his own on missions. He lives with his family in Texas, is in the bishopric of his ward there, and has flown in from Texas to be here." The son then came forward, and we embraced one another.

She concluded, "It has taken a lot of planning as well as time and money and effort to get us all together. For many years we have had a great desire to have this feast with you before we die. We wanted to tell you of the great blessings the Lord has given us since that marvelous evening in Pangai, fifty years ago." She then bore her testimony and sat down.

During her story, long-latent memories had exploded into my consciousness and I could remember every detail, so as I stood to respond I had difficulty knowing where to begin. I acknowledged the Lord's goodness in all of our lives and said that He expects us to continue living in faith and service forever. I thanked them for their efforts and sacrifice in bringing this feast of gratitude to pass. I spoke of an even greater feast of gratitude we will attend in the future if we live worthy of it. I reminded everyone of the opportunity to practice and prepare for that great feast by worthily attending the weekly sacramental feast of repentance, forgiveness, acknowledgment, and renewed determination to be better.

Later, I checked my journal and found a brief entry: "*God blessed Sione's mother with faith and allowed him to be healed. Several baptisms followed. We are very busy. God is blessing us abundantly.*"

THE TRUMPET

At a Tongan gathering a middle-aged Tongan man came up to me and said, "You likely don't know me, but I surely know you. As a teenage boy, I attended your school in Ha'apai whenever I could. I was not a member, and my family was very opposed to the Church, so I had to sneak away from my school to go to yours. I especially tried to be there to hear you play the trumpet during music class."

I only vaguely remembered this man, but I clearly recalled that there had always been extra students during music class. He continued: "I don't remember a lot from the school, but how I remember your trumpet playing! I wanted to play just like you. When you left for America my parents sent me to another school on another island because they didn't want me to associate anymore with the Mormons.

"My granduncle was a member of the Church, and it was through him and your trumpet that I became a member. My granduncle told me that you wanted to leave your trumpet in Tonga, but your father asked you to bring it home and he would send another one to leave with the school. [That original trumpet was used in the film *The Other Side of Heaven*.]

"Just before you left, this other trumpet arrived, and you gave it to my granduncle, who was a good trumpet player. You

John with his trumpet at a Scouting event in Pangai, Ha'apai, Tonga.

probably don't remember, but as you gave the trumpet to my granduncle you told him to be free in letting others learn to play. Then you specifically told him that you felt I would want to learn to play the trumpet. He was to teach me—on the condition that before each lesson, I would listen to a gospel discussion that he would give me. My parents were still opposed to the Church but agreed to this arrangement, as it was a way for me to learn to play the trumpet.

"Over time I learned to play the trumpet, but more importantly, I learned the truth of the gospel of Jesus Christ. When I turned eighteen years old, I joined the Church. Later I served a mission and married in the temple, and we have a wonderful posterity who are active in the Church. We live in the eastern part of the United States now and are deeply grateful for the gospel in our lives. Thanks for the trumpet, and thanks for your parting words to my granduncle."

Seeing and hearing the fulfillment of those long-forgotten words inspired by God nearly fifty years ago—so simple, yet so important—I could only weep with gratitude. As we tearfully embraced, I sensed a smile and seemed to hear the clear sound of a trumpet coming from the depths of eternity.

THE BLESSING

A widowed mother whom I had known in Tonga asked if I could please perform the temple sealing of her youngest son. I arranged my schedule to do so.

The son had been through many winding paths, some of which led downward. But through the faith of his mother and the help of friends and priesthood leaders, he now knelt worthily in that sacred room as eternal promises, responsibilities, and blessings were given and received. The Spirit of the Lord was so strong that his deceased father was able to make his happiness known.

That evening a marvelous traditional Tongan feast and dance was held for the newlyweds. At the appropriate time, the mother arose and said she wanted to explain how she had come to join the Church about fifty years before. This is her story:

"My husband and I moved to a distant island in Tonga where we met Kolipoki. He did everything he could to help me join the Church and to encourage my husband to become more active. He was not very successful at either, at least for a while. Kolipoki

Tongan Saints in the 1950s.

and his companion, Feki, and a few members decided they needed a new church house, so they set about building one with their own hands. There was no monetary expense, but the cost in labor was high. In Tonga everyone helps build another's place of worship, so we helped. On the first Sunday after the chapel was finished we all came to the dedication.

"It was a proud day for Kolipoki to have a new building full of people to listen to his preaching. He knew it was a one-time opportunity to teach and testify to us, since those who were not members would return to their own churches the following Sunday.

"Kolipoki was teaching the Sunday School lesson, when suddenly I began to feel very ill. I was expecting a baby, but not for many weeks. I left the meeting and went home. I lay down to rest, and the thought came to me: 'I need some help, but no one will come. My husband will probably stay at the new chapel listening to Kolipoki. This is too big of a day for them to worry about me.'

"Soon I heard a rustle outside, and in walked Kolipoki and my husband. 'What are you doing here?' I asked. Kolipoki responded, 'I could tell you were ill, and had a feeling you needed some help. I turned the lesson over to someone else and we are here.' I cried and cried and asked for forgiveness. 'For what?' Kolipoki asked. I replied, 'I guess only I know. Please give me a blessing.' You did, and I was made well. I then asked what I needed to do to be baptized. You had the answer, and soon I was baptized and my husband became more active.

"We moved from Tonga and eventually settled in the United States. I am now in Utah as a widow. With the sealing of this son, all of our children have been sealed in the temple and are active in the Church. Thank you, Kolipoki, for leaving your Sunday School lesson and a chapel full of people to come and give me a blessing. It has meant more than life itself to me. Thank you for what it has brought into my life and that of my family. Even though my husband is beyond the veil, we know we are sealed together forever. I still wonder: How did you know, and why did you leave so many people to come and give me a blessing?"

As I stood to respond, I felt impressed to answer her question by simply saying, "At the time, I felt it was the right thing to do." Then, looking at her and at her large posterity gathered there, I said, "I still feel the same today."

THE FAST

During a Tongan event in California the bishop had all the newly baptized and activated members stand. It was an impressive group. They all radiated love and appreciation for their good bishop. I expressed gratitude for the bishop and his good influence. He said, "I would like to tell you how I became active in the Church."

He explained that it was through the events surrounding our son John Enoch's birth and illness in Tonga that he had gained a testimony. Our first son, John Enoch, was born when we were serving in Tonga, and he experienced several episodes of severe illness, culminating in a life-threatening situation where he could not keep anything down and was on the verge of death. As I sat at his side, a large delegation of Tongan Saints arrived and informed me that they had been fasting and praying.

This bishop in California had been a teenager at the time these events were taking place. When his mother told him that all the Saints were fasting for John Enoch and asked him to participate, he replied, "No, thanks." Fasting was not part of this teenager's life. In fact, he was rapidly slipping into inactivity.

Something touched him, however, and the next day, without saying anything to anyone, he ate nothing. He said he had never been able to fast before, but for some reason he did so now with joy, feeling a real sense of purpose. That evening when the

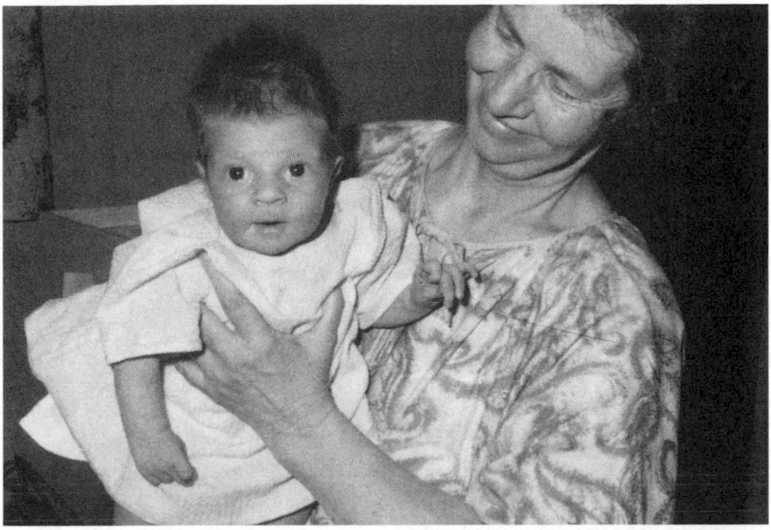

John Enoch and Grandma Groberg, shortly before John Enoch became ill.

members throughout Tonga, Fiji, and Niue broke their fast with a prayer for John Enoch, that young man quietly slipped into the back of their chapel. During the prayer he felt such a strong spirit of goodness that he knew the Church was true and that the powers of faith, fasting, prayer, and priesthood were real. It thrilled him to the bone. He received a personal witness that God had acknowledged his fasting and the fasting of thousands of others, and that He would answer by allowing John Enoch to live—which He did.

This young man returned to activity, served a mission, married in the temple, served as a bishop, raised a great family, and was now serving as a bishop again. He concluded, "Elder Groberg, it all started when I fasted and prayed for John Enoch. I'm glad John Enoch is doing well and has children of his own. I'm glad you are here today. I know how grandparents feel towards grandchildren. I hope these quilts help show our love for you and Jean and your family, especially your grandchildren." (We had a lot of grandchildren, and they had a quilt for each one.)

As I returned home, I realized more than ever how God can and does cause good things to happen when there is true love and faith and a sincere desire to help others. Even the sickness of a baby can be paired with the rebelliousness of a teenager to bring about a change of course so both can live.

* * *

If we live our lives so we can hear and heed the promptings of the Spirit, there is no limit to the good God can accomplish through us. Part of living worthily is to not seek or desire recognition, but to humbly obey spiritual promptings, knowing that, whether we are aware or not, God will bring the increase in His own way and in His own time.

I know that if there is purity of purpose and desire along with diligent effort, anyone, anytime, anywhere, under any circumstance can become an instrument in the Lord's hands to bring about marvelous changes that are nothing short of miracles.

Chapter 8

The Poison Fish

An older Tongan gentleman asked Jean and me and our family to come to his grandson's first birthday celebration. In Tongan culture, the importance of the first birthday dates back generations, to when many children died before reaching the age of one. If a child reached his or her first birthday, there was cause for great celebration, as there was now a good likelihood that the child would live to maturity.

The birthday celebration was the excuse, but the grandfather indicated there was something else he needed to tell me, and he wanted all of his family to be there when he did. I agreed to attend. In typical Tongan style, they had gone all out with a huge feast, large crowds, long speeches, and lots of dancing, singing, and music. When all this wound down, the grandfather rose in great solemnity to speak. Everyone paid strict attention.

He spoke in the old Tongan poetic form, using allegorical words and phrases that created an aura of beauty and mystery and held everyone spellbound. He talked of an event that had happened many years ago and the great impact it had had on him and his family.

Display of quilts given as gifts for each of our grandchildren at a birthday celebration.

He explained that he was an experienced sailor in Ha'apai, Tonga, during the time I was there as a missionary. As a young man he did not like the Mormons and took every occasion he could to undermine my preaching and make it difficult for me. I was serving as district president and needed to make frequent visits to the many islands in Ha'apai. Since there were not many boats in Ha'apai at that time, this man and I frequently ended up on the same boat.

As I sailed from island to island, I generally tried to preach to those on board. This man did his best not to listen, disrupting me often and generally refuting whatever I said.

On one particular voyage to a group of small islands some distance from our home in Pangai, we were becalmed several times. The lack of wind extended what normally would have been a two-day trip into the fourth day. Everyone suffered from the shortage of food and water. In the late afternoon we found ourselves close to an uninhabited island, and I suggested to the captain that we go ashore, spend the night, and hope for some wind in the morning. He agreed, and as we slowly drifted to the island, we caught a good-sized fish.

Typical Tongan sailboat in a calm sea.

The man telling the story, and some others on the boat that day, realized that it was a poison fish but decided not to say anything. Before long, we were ashore, had a fire going, and were cooking the fish. The man thought: "I will just let the Mormon missionary eat the fish and die, and we'll be rid of that problem." But as the fish was about ready to eat, his conscience got the best of him, and he blurted out, "Kolipoki, that is a poison fish; don't eat it or you will die."

According to his memory, I looked at him and said, "Whether it is poisonous or not, I do not know, but this I do know—we need the strength to make it back home. I am going to say a prayer to God and ask Him to bless this food. In case you are right, I will ask God to change the fish from *kona* to *melie* (a poisonous one to a sweet one). If during the prayer God tells me not to eat it, I won't; otherwise, I will and so will the others."

He recalled that during the prayer he scoffed but also felt something he had not felt before: respect for a Mormon elder. The prayer concluded and we ate the fish—all except the man telling the story. The others felt inclined to believe me, but he continued to doubt. He observed me carefully through the night, but it passed without incident. A good wind came up in the morning, and we made it back home before sunset the next evening. He said he watched me for several days, but I seemed to stay healthy.

Shortly after this incident, I completed my mission and prepared to leave for home. Nearly everyone on the island wished me well in one way or another. There were *laka lakas,* feasts, speeches, as well as individual farewells. This man came to me and simply asked how I was feeling. I replied, "I feel wonderful. I am sad to leave the people of Tonga, but happy that God has preserved my life and blessed me with faith and testimony, and given me the opportunity to share these truths with others." (I had no clear recollection of this exchange, but it was indelibly inscribed in his memory.)

He continued his account by telling how he stood on the shore and watched my sailboat gradually sink below the horizon. Then, overcome with emotion, tears flowing freely, he knelt and asked for forgiveness. When he arose, he returned to his home and told his wife and young children he was going to become a Mormon and hoped they would follow. He did, and they followed.

Now, as he told the story many years later, he felt those same emotions. Tears flowed down his wrinkled face as he thanked me for eating a poison fish made sweet by God, thus bringing light and life to him and his family. He said they had long since moved from Tonga, but all of his family were active members of the Church, and more than thirty of his descendants had served missions. He expressed gratitude for the temple marriages and the many other blessings he and his family had received. As he concluded with his testimony there was profound silence, except for muffled sobs and wiping of tears everywhere. Even the year-old baby was quiet.

As he sat down, every eye turned to where I was sitting, and I knew it was my responsibility to give a response. My emotions were very tender also, and I was still trying to sort things out in my mind. When he began his oration, I had nothing but the faintest flickering of a memory of those events, which obviously had not seemed like any big deal to me at the time. They hadn't found their way into my journal, as many other events had not, usually because I could not write in a bouncing boat with salt spray all over. When I finally did reach land, I had other things to worry about and often forgot about these events.

I thanked this man and his family for their faithfulness, encouraged them to continue on the gospel path, and assured them of eternal blessings as they did. I acknowledged that this incident had been a bigger thing to him than it had been to me back then, but I was very happy knowing the Lord had seen fit to use this event to help him and his family come to the truth. I testified that the Lord not only uses anyone, at anytime, but also any circumstance, anywhere, to help individuals and families come unto Him and accomplish His purposes.

I bore testimony that God lives and has all power and loves His children with an infinite love that is beyond our comprehension. I testified then, and testify now, that God can and will change a poison fish to a sweet one and a doubting heart to a believing one, if there is sufficient faith.

Chapter 9

HOW BEAUTIFUL . . .

We had just finished a stake conference in Nuku'alofa, Tonga. The foyer and hallways were full of smiling people wanting to visit and share their joy in the gospel. I wanted to linger longer, but the stake president urged me along as there was a plane to catch.

Just as we were disengaging from the crowd someone grabbed my arm and spun me around. Before I had time to think, I found myself face to face with a short, heavy-set, very strong, elderly woman. Her whole face was one huge smile. Her last remaining tooth glistened like a brilliant diamond solitaire from her open mouth. She looked at me carefully, then grasped my head and neck, pulled me down to her, and gave me a Tongan kiss (cheek to cheek, with a soft but definite nasal inhaling).

Startled, I wondered: "Who is this old woman? What does she want? What should I do?" But the instant she inhaled, a distant memory rushed to the front of my mind. (Is there an aroma to love?)

"Asi—Asi Hoatatau!" I cried.

It had been years since I had seen Asi. My physical eyes saw an older woman, spent and tired, but my heart saw a bright, young branch president's wife full of life and love.

As I returned her Tongan kiss, I said: "Asi, Asi, *'oku ke kei mo'ui!*" (Asi, Asi, you're still alive!) Through tears of joy, she replied, "*Kei mo'ui au.*" (I'm still alive.)

Suddenly she released her grip on my neck and slipped to my feet. Before I knew what was happening, she was rubbing and kissing my feet through my sandals. Her tears fell freely, soaking into my stockings. Between sobs she looked up and said: "*Ho ongo va'e. Kua na sai? Kuo na sai. Malo'ae'Otua.*" (Your feet. Are they fine? They are fine. Thanks be to God.)

Vivid memories and deep emotions stirred within me and I barely managed the response: "Yes, my feet are fine. Thanks be to God and thanks be to you!"

She continued crying and rubbing my feet while repeating over and over: "*Ho ongo va'e—kuo na sai. Kuo na sai. Faka'ofa'ofa ho va'e.*" (Your feet—they are fine. They are fine. Your feet are beautiful.) My mind was really whirling now. I sensed something important was happening. I strained to understand what it was.

Scriptures and pictures flooded into my mind, and I seemed to hear the words of Isaiah through the Prophet Joseph Smith saying: "How beautiful upon the mountains are the feet of those that bring glad tidings of good things, and that say unto Zion: Behold, thy God reigneth!" (Doctrine and Covenants 128:19). I wondered, "Am I bearing glad tidings and doing good things? Are my feet beautiful?" I heard Paul pleading, "[Have] your feet shod with the preparation of the gospel of peace" (Ephesians 6:15), and I wondered, "Are they?" Then I heard Peter when the Savior prepared to wash his feet, first protesting, then pleading for Him to wash not only his feet but his whole body (see John 13:8–9). I wondered, "Am I as anxious to be washed clean by the Savior?"

I looked at my feet. Asi was still rubbing them. I suppose I was a little embarrassed and asked her to stand. She would not move, so I bent down and lifted her up. As I gazed into her aged, weather-worn face, I remembered all she had done for me many years ago. The memory filled my heart and mind to overflowing, and I was unable to move.

Time stood still. Logically, I knew we were in a hurry and needed to catch the plane, but that didn't seem to matter now. I was in a different element of time and space—no longer in the midst of a crowd, no longer worried about time or schedules, no longer pushing to go anywhere. I was back on the small island of Niuatoputapu as a young missionary.*

In vivid detail I relived that morning when I awoke and, as I stood up, heard a terrible squishing sound, felt sharp pain, and saw blood oozing from my feet. My feet! What had happened? I cried out in alarm. My companion, Feki, went for help and came running back with the branch president's wife, Asi. They looked at my feet and shook their heads in deep concern. Unawares, I had slept with my feet uncovered, and the rats had eaten the callouses off of the soles of my feet, so as I stood, the weight of my body caused the remaining thin skin to split in many places. This was serious trouble. There were neither doctors nor antibiotics on the island. What could we do? Feki was pale. Asi cried. I saw fear in their faces and heard them whisper of potentially fatal consequences.

Imploringly, I looked at them. As though reading my thoughts, they looked at each other, then at me, then smiled. The concern in their faces was replaced by absolute assurance. I felt the power of pure love and deep faith coming from them. It glowed from their eyes and seemed to say: "You are on God's errand. You are our missionary. We'll take care of you. If it be God's will that you live, we will do whatever is necessary to get

---

*See *In the Eye of the Storm,* pp. 68–70.

you well." I knew their love and faith were powerful, even unconquerable. How that buoyed me up!

Following a priesthood blessing, they said the infection must be stopped. There were two options: searing the soles of my feet with a hot bush knife, or letting the sun do the searing. The sun sounded better. After carefully washing my feet with special Tongan oils, they carried me outside, tied to a chair, and laid me on the ground so my head and body were down but the soles of my feet were facing the sun.

At first the sun felt good, but after a while it hurt terribly. Hour after hour, day after day, the merciless, burning, hurting, healing, purifying rays of the sun beat down on my feet. During all those long hours Asi faithfully rubbed my feet with herbs and oils, while encouraging, smiling, praying, laughing, assuring, bringing me drinks, and adjusting my position so my feet were always facing the sun and my face and body were in the shade. Dear Asi.

When the soles of my feet were finally burned to the proverbial crisp, Asi announced that the searing was sufficient. Then came the waiting. Sometimes I waited patiently, sometimes not so patiently. At times I was scared and questioned whether this strange treatment would really work and eliminate the dreaded infection. But when I looked into Feki's eyes, saw Asi's smile, and felt my family's prayers, I knew it would—it had to. What a blessing it was to feel Asi's determination. No matter the odds, I knew her love and faith would prove more powerful than the rat's infection. What peace that knowledge gave me!

One day Asi announced that it was time for me to take a few steps. This word spread quickly, and soon a crowd of curious onlookers gathered. This was a big event for a small island. Asi and Feki carried me outside. They helped me stand, then moved away. After not walking for such a long time, my legs and feet were stiff and sore. Teetering and with great trepidation I looked around. Many eyes were fastened on me and my feet. Most of them were shining with hope and encouragement, but a few showed signs of doubt and even disdain. I looked again at Feki and Asi. Their smiles came back with the absolute assurance that I could and would take those steps. Though I stood alone, I did not feel alone.

After what seemed a long time, I took a deep breath and moved my feet. One step, two steps, three steps. I could walk! A giant thrill reverberated through my whole body as I experienced the joy of walking again! There was a chorus of "oohs" and "aahs" and spontaneous clapping. But above everything else I heard one magical, high-pitched squeal of joy. Instinctively I looked at Asi and saw her hands tightly squeezed to the front of her face with tears streaming down her cheeks. I was full of joy, but as I looked at Asi, I wondered, who felt the most joy?

I looked at my feet again and wondered: What brought about the healing? Was it the sun? the herbs? the oil? the rubbing? the priesthood blessing? the prayers of my family? Feki's faith? Asi's love? Undoubtedly all played a part, but at that moment I understood that it was Asi's pure love that had held everything together and allowed the miracle of healing to take place.*

I understood how Asi's actions, which were motivated by pure love and deep faith, had moved beyond the limits of time. I could see how when anyone acts out of pure love, eternal forces

---

*I had trouble with my feet for many years after my mission. Finally a specialist found that I had skin cancer on the bottom of my feet. This is extremely rare, so he asked if anything unusual had happened. I told him of the sun-burning treatment in Tonga many years earlier and he felt sure that was the cause. He said the Tongans were wiser than they may have known, as the ultraviolet rays of the sun are very effective in fighting infection. He felt that under the circumstances, that particular treatment had likely saved my life, as otherwise the infection may not have been controlled. He removed the skin cancer, and my feet have been fine since.

Asi, on right, with her husband and daughter.

are set in motion that will not stop until the full measure of their decreed course is achieved.

Then I thought: Isn't it pure love that allows all healing to take place? Even the ultimate healing from death and sin? As I thought of this, time stood still again and I found myself in another crowd. I watched as, through the press of people, a faithful woman touched a hem and healing took place. It was beautiful! I understood that the only actions that really count are those done out of pure love and deep faith, which anyone can perform, anytime, anywhere. Everything that is not incorporated in God's love eventually burns itself out and ceases to exist. Love never fails but endures forever.

More scenes flowed through my mind. I saw a woman pouring a bottle of precious oil on tired feet, paying no heed to those who chided her for being wasteful, but following her feelings of pure love and receiving the Master's smile of approval. "It was that Mary which anointed the Lord with ointment, and wiped his feet with her hair, whose brother Lazarus was sick" (John 11:2). Yes, He would save her and her brother and all who act out of pure love.

I felt His plea: "If I then, your Lord and Master, have washed your feet; ye also ought to wash one another's feet" (John 13:14). Again, I thought of Asi and how she had cared for my feet, giving no thought to the smell or appearance of severely burned flesh, but acting out of pure love. I thought of mothers and fathers changing smelly diapers, cleaning up spilt milk, holding sick children, nursing the aged or sick. I thought of others who, like the good Samaritan, willingly serve those they don't even know, in homeless shelters, in work projects, cleaning up from disasters, and in many other ways.

I realized there would be no meaningful existence without God's love. Yes, love comes as a gift from God, but its power in us is rooted in the sacrifices we are willing to make for that love. We must learn to act out of pure love (including fully forgiving) as the Savior did and does and always will. Therein is eternal power and progress. Therein is all beauty, life, and light. Therein is the essence of godliness.

In the midst of these reveries, I felt someone jostle me and realized I was back in Nuku'alofa still surrounded by a large crowd of smiling people. The power of love, however, had shielded Asi and me from the intrusion of the crowd and the moving of the clock. Even though I did not want to move, the stake president pulled my arm and said, "We must hurry." Slowly, reluctantly, my mind returned to the crowded foyer. I saw Asi standing next to me, searching my very soul with a penetrating look of love. I smiled at her. She looked like an angel—she was an angel. I gave her a final Tongan kiss and bid her farewell. She smiled and quietly melted into the crowd.

I thought of Asi often in the weeks and months following our unexpected reunion at that stake conference in Tonga. However, as time and events pressed on, the conscious memory of that visit faded. Then one day I received a message that Asi had passed away at home on her beloved island of Niuatoputapu. I immediately sought a secluded place where I could ponder, pray, and remember.

As I did, I again felt Asi's presence. In a very real way, I saw her smile, heard her laugh, and felt her tenderly rubbing my feet. I remembered that day in Tonga when I took those first uncertain steps on my newly healed feet. How radiantly Asi shone, with her hands squeezed tightly over her face. This time, however, I felt something new. For the first time I became aware of how often Asi had been very tired but, through steadfast determination, refused to slow down or show her weariness. In all those days of rubbing and encouraging I had never once sensed her fatigue, yet now I could see and feel it clearly. My heart cried out, "Well done, Asi! You didn't complain. You kept your tiredness from me, but God knew all along."

I came to understand that part of the beauty of a Christlike character consists of continuing to love and help even when you are tired. Asi knew that something needed to be done and she did it without letting others know how tired she was—not even a sigh. I realized that it is possible to love so deeply and so purely that the hurt and pain and tiredness involved in the expression of that love are "swallowed up in the joy of Christ" (see Alma 31:38).

I thought of things I should have done but didn't because I was "too tired," or because I "had done enough," or because I felt "someone else should do it." I was embarrassed by those realizations, yet encouraged by the assurance that God is good to forgive and offer us new opportunities. If we love and trust Him sufficiently, He will always give us the strength needed to achieve whatever tasks lie before us. When our trials seem too long or too hard, we must remember that only God can say how much is enough, for only He knows the growth that we can gain by pushing beyond the tiredness and the pain.

Hong Kong from the air.

I thought this would likely be the end of my experiences with Asi. However, I learned that good things never end, true love has no termination, and God's help is forever. Many years later, I was walking through downtown Hong Kong with nothing particular on my mind when I suddenly felt the presence of Asi. While totally unexpected, her presence was very real. I was excited to visit with her once again. Everything seemed so natural that I immediately began a conversation with her in Tongan. She asked about my feet. I told her that they were fine and that I often walked to work. She smiled. For some reason, I had a great desire to show her around Hong Kong. She sensed my desire and said, "*Ta o!*" (Let's go!)

Somehow we were freed from the restraints of mortal motion and moved about with ease and certainty. Asi appeared amazed at the powerful cars, the rapid trains, the tall buildings, the beautiful bridges, the intricate road systems, and the huge numbers of people and goods everywhere. I took her to a large hotel where, from a moving glass elevator, I showed her a beautiful mural, fifteen stories high. Her eyes were wide with wonder and amazement.

Then, in the midst of my enthusiasm, I looked at Asi and could tell that she needed to leave. She smiled, but before leaving she looked at me carefully, first at my feet, then into my eyes. In her distinctive Tongan, she said, "Kolipoki, what great power, what constant activity, what huge structures, what beautiful murals you have here. Thank you for showing them to me. I have just one question: Do these things help you love people more?" Her voice and eyes were filled with certainty and with love. I knew she loved me and wanted to help me. Her question sank deep into my soul. I knew the answer, but as I started to respond by saying, "Not really," I looked and couldn't find her. She was gone.

I realized I was standing on a sidewalk near a busy intersection in bustling downtown Hong Kong. I looked frantically around, but all I could see were giant buildings, swarming people, powerful cars, and intense activity. The whole experience must have happened instantaneously, as things were just as they had been before and no one was staring at me. Even though she was no longer with me, I decided to answer her anyway. As I did, the buildings, the cars, the streets, and every physical thing seemed to fade away, and again I could see Asi's smiling face nodding her approval. Instinctively I whispered, *"Malo e tokoni. Ofa atu. Ta toki fe'iloaki. Alu a."* (Thanks for the help. I love you. We'll meet again. Good-bye.)

It was clear to me that even though she had lived her whole life on one small island (except her trip to the New Zealand Temple), Asi had learned more and knew more about what is important in eternity than many of us do who have seen the wide world and busied our lives with constant coming and going. Life is a series of opportunities to learn to love purely and to show

View from the Hubble Telescope—going on forever.

that love by our actions—anytime, anywhere, under any circumstance. Each opportunity taken opens broader, deeper, and more challenging vistas; each opportunity rejected decreases (or at least delays) those grander vistas. What a great lesson she taught me! When anyone acts out of pure love to help others in a truly unselfish way, that love sets in motion eternal waves of beauty, goodness, and blessings that never end.

Chapter 10

A TEMPLE IN TONGA!

A temple in Tonga! The long-awaited, much-anticipated blessing was finally being realized for the faithful Saints of Tonga. Only those who have worked with a people as long and closely as I had can appreciate the emotions that filled my soul upon hearing this news. For many years I had watched the Lord's work move steadily forward among the Polynesians. Now He was blessing them with their own temples! The Lord had heard and answered the prayers of countless faithful island people from both sides of the veil. What a blessing that there were now temples throughout Polynesia. As I think back to the many marvelous events that took place during this time, a few experiences were particularly memorable.

OPEN HOUSE

In 1983 we were living in Bountiful, Utah, but assigned to supervise the work of the Church in the Pacific Islands. As part of that responsibility, I was in charge of the open house and planning for the dedication of the temple in Tonga. Jean and I conducted many VIP tours of the temple. The people who went

Throngs of Tongans came day after day to the temple open house.

through included the King and Queen, members of the Royal Family, government leaders, and officials from other churches, among others. There were dozens of tours, and an amazing number of Tongans visited the temple. What heartwarming and eternally significant conversations we had! As with all temple open houses, questions were asked, prayers were answered, hearts were touched, and eternal truths were explained. As a result, seeds of truth were planted and many long-buried testimonies were reawakened. We collected an abundance of referrals, and many people joined the Church largely because of what they experienced at the open house.

Of the many groups we conducted through the temple open house, one in particular will forever be etched in my heart. At that time, the nation of Tonga was generally peaceful, with very little violent crime. Occasionally someone got drunk and raised some havoc, but for the most part society was quite tranquil. There were no prisons as we know them, just designated enclosures with a single strand of barbed wire surrounding them. Many of the inmates were there because they had failed to pay their taxes or committed some other similar violation. Often people were sent to prison to work in government gardens until their debts were paid. So, in a sense, the inmates were not really "criminals," as we use the term.

Without my knowledge, President Tonga Toutai Paletu'a, who had been called by President Spencer W. Kimball to be the temple's first president, had made arrangements with one of the wardens to bring a group of these so-called "prisoners" to an open house tour. Other than their casual attire and the presence of a couple of unarmed guards with them, they appeared much like the other groups going through the open house.

Toward the end of the day I was taking a group through when I noticed President Paletu'a and his group. I was a little surprised, but felt no concern, as I had full confidence in him. After I finished with my group, I looked around the temple to see if I could find President Paletu'a and his group. I found them in the baptismal area. The scene that I witnessed was so spiritually penetrating that I could hardly move or even breathe. The display of beauty emanating from this group that it transfixed me right where I stood.

The "prisoners" were standing in the back aisle facing the baptismal font. President Paletu'a was speaking to them. Their eyes were fastened on him. They were listening with complete attention and deep reverence as he read from Doctrine and Covenants 128:22: "Courage, brethren; . . . Let your hearts rejoice, and be exceedingly glad . . . for the prisoners shall go free." When he finished reading, he bore his testimony, then stood there with great power and majesty. All of the men, including the guards, were in tears there in the Lord's house. As I looked at that group of "prisoners," I could literally feel their belief in the truths that had just been explained. They truly wanted to be free—in more ways than one—and they knew that through the Savior's atonement and resurrection, and by obedience to gospel ordinances and principles, they could be. Their gratitude for the Savior and the path laid out for them, along with their determination to obey Him, was as strong as a pulsating heartbeat and could not be denied.

I probably should have closed the door and stepped out, but I couldn't. I was glued to the spot by the marvelous light of truth and gratitude for the Savior flowing so freely from those in that room. In a way, I sensed that this scene and these feelings were but a prelude of things to come—here and hereafter. It was as though I was in an element beyond this world. It was so beautiful and so satisfying that I wished it to last forever.

I'm not sure when they left the room, for the reverent hush continued as the "prisoners" and their guards filed out to their waiting vans. Each one expressed deep, heartfelt appreciation for all they had seen, heard, and felt. I watched President Paletu'a shaking hands and giving hugs to the departing group. He looked like an angel—confidently standing in humble dignity, dressed in white, smiling, encouraging, uplifting. He knew he had followed the promptings of the Lord's Spirit and done that which the Savior would have done, had He been there. From the look in President Paletu'a's eyes and the glow from his very being, I knew in a way He had been.

Years later, I asked President Paletu'a if he had followed through with the men from the prison. He reported that the few who had been less-active members of the Church at the time were now active. The others had all been baptized and were likewise active. Truly, the Lord performs wonders in mysterious ways. How grateful I was to have been permitted to stand on the periphery and catch a glimpse of the towering testimony of those faithful descendants of Joseph!

DEDICATION

Shortly after the open house, President Gordon B. Hinckley and a few other Brethren came for the dedication. Each session was so fulfilling, so full of the Spirit, and so emotional, I cannot adequately put into words the feelings I had. Suffice it to say, there was more than just a perceived connection between the faithful Tongan members physically in the temple and those watching from the other side of the veil.

Anyone who is acquainted with the Tongan people knows how much they enjoy singing and how beautifully they do it. Song and music are a big part of how they express themselves and their culture. When the hand-selected choir sang during the first dedication session, the connections across the veil became vibrantly evident. There was room for about thirty to sing in the choir. In preparation for the dedication, they had practiced and practiced. When the director felt they had the harmony and phrasing just right, he insisted on practicing again with the room

Elder Groberg with temple presidency.
Left to right: Semisi Vaha'i Tonga (first counselor), Elder Groberg, President Tonga Toutai Paletu'a, Filimone Fie'eiki (second counselor).

full of people so that he could make the needed adjustments, no matter how small. The director and the choir had put forth every effort to have as nearly perfect a sound as was humanly possible. When they sang, their preparation was acknowledged in heaven, and choirs from above joined them as they honored the Lord in a perfectly seamless wave of praise that resounded through time and eternity.

Those phrases of praise glorified His name, purified the singers, and transformed all those present who had eyes to see, ears to hear, and hearts to feel. Light and truth connected the heavens and the earth for a brief period. (Or are they always joined, but only rarely do we see, hear, and feel it?) Through temples it is literally possible to dissolve the lines between the past, present, and future, as well as "here" and "there." When we sense these connections, it gives us courage and desire to do better and be better. The Spirit was so strong, the preparation so deep, and the closeness to heaven so accepted by this believing people that I could fully relate to Nephi's description of manifestations that "tongue cannot speak . . . neither can be written by man . . ." (3 Nephi 19:32).

TEMPLE WORK

The morning after the final dedication session in Tonga, ordinance work began. The day was filled with miracles, great faith, hard work, long hours, and much love and patience. We started early in the morning and went late into the evening. There were many questions, much newness, and great desire, especially on the part of the dozens of couples and their families to be sealed. Jean and I, along with all of the temple workers, were fully occupied every moment of the day. Taking time to eat or rest was not feasible, nor was it in our thoughts. Regardless of the physical strain on our bodies, during that glorious day we neither hungered, thirsted, nor tired. The Lord's Spirit is the great healer and the great peace-giver in more ways than one. How grateful I was for the skilled temple department staff who so kindly and efficiently guided us through that remarkable time.

As we neared the end of the day, I noticed that there were but two couples waiting to be sealed. All the paperwork was supposedly in order, and soon they too would receive the blessings they had patiently waited and prepared for. We were confident that President Paletu'a and others would finish properly, so Jean and I left to return to our room. As we went out through the front door, a worker pointed to a group of seven young children dressed in white whose broad smiles and longing eyes said without words, "When is our turn?" We asked how long they had been waiting. They explained that they had been there since early morning. Their parents had entered the temple before breakfast and told them to wait until they were called. (There was no children's waiting room at that time.)

The older girls had patiently cared for the others as they waited and waited and waited. They had had nothing to eat, but did not complain. I asked who their parents were and returned to the temple to check on what had happened.

There was now only one couple left in the waiting area. I asked their name—they were the parents of the children waiting outside. I asked how long they had been there. "Since early this morning," they replied. "We handed in our paperwork and were told to wait here until our names were called." I went to the recording area and asked about this couple. "Sorry," they replied. "We have no record of them as no paperwork has been submitted."

Acting on a prompting, I said, "Let's check through all the completed paperwork to make sure." We began searching through the large number of completed forms. Partway through, one set felt a little thicker than the rest. We checked and, sure enough, attached to the bottom were the missing forms! The couple's papers had not been processed because they had accidentally been caught by a paper clip on the forms above.

Quickly we called the couple and brought the children in, and shortly thereafter this precious family was sealed for time and all eternity. As soon as the year-old baby got near his mother, he grabbed onto her, determined never to let go! With tear-filled eyes we all felt a desire to hold fast to our own loved ones and never let go—grateful for the saving ordinances and sealing powers in holy temples of God that made such a thing possible.

What joy, what gratitude this family felt! Their waiting all day seemed nothing to them. The only thing that mattered was that they were now an eternal family. They had waited patiently on the Lord and realized his promise, "How great things thou hast prepared for him that waiteth for thee" (Doctrine and Covenants 133:45). What a lesson!

I wondered: Where else do people—parents and children—wait patiently all day to be called and told it is their turn, never complaining or even asking, just trusting in the Lord and His servants, knowing that only when it is their turn will they go, not before. I thought of how many other families are waiting, waiting, waiting (on both sides of the veil), and realized again how much more work there is to do.

Yes, marvelous things occur when we yield our hearts and minds to the Lord, especially in connection with temple work. Eternally important changes are made in the temple as we soften our hearts, determine to follow God's laws with more fervor, and become more Christlike in our nature. Temples bring eternal blessings to everyone, everywhere across all eternity. Hearts are softened, latent seeds of truth begin to sprout, prisoners are set free, praises are sung with more harmony and meaning, connections between here and there are more evident, families are sealed for eternity, promises are made, and joy becomes a reality, now and forever!

Chapter 11

KELEPI

I have learned that the Lord honors those who through their lives have honored Him. He does it in different ways for different people, but always in a way fitting to the individual. I have learned that God is pleased when we honor those who have lived and loved and served well in this life. One such person who always honored the Lord was Kelepi La'iafe Ikatauimoana Talakai. God not only honored him as he moved to the other side, but blessed countless others as He did so. Here is the story of Kelepi and how the Lord paid a final earthly honor to him.

Kelepi's body was small, but his name was big and his heart was even bigger. As a young missionary I learned what a good captain and faithful helper he was. He had been "the Lord's wind" literally, rowing our boat when we were becalmed and prayed for help on the ocean, but he had also filled that role figuratively in more ways than one. When I returned to Tonga as mission president, he was obviously older, but still working hard. Motorboats were by then replacing sailboats, so his special sailing skills were in less demand. He still volunteered to help anytime and in any way he could. He attended meetings, shared his food and drink, and was always dependable.

Kelepi lived next door to the chapel in Pangai, Ha'apai, Tonga. He kept his house and yard and that of the church neat and clean. The magnificent coral wall that had earlier surrounded the chapel had been constructed mainly by Kelepi. When the decision was made to replace that wooden chapel with a new block one, the architect directed that the old coral wall must come down and be replaced by a chain-link fence. Many local people objected, but Kelepi said, "If that is what the Brethren want, I am the first to support the decision."

After returning from serving as mission president, I lost track of Kelepi for several years. Then one day I received an assignment as a Regional Representative to hold a midweek district conference in Ha'apai, Tonga, between two weekend stake conferences in Nuku'alofa, Tonga. I was thrilled with that assignment and happy to find that an airport had just been opened in Ha'apai.

It was fun to fly to Ha'apai. The distance that had taken me twenty hours or more to cover by sailboat was now traversed in less than one hour. The place on the island where they built the runway was so narrow that the airstrip literally went from the ocean on one side to the ocean on the other side. Though not large in size, it was adequate for the small airplane that flew there.

In Ha'apai we held several marvelous missionary meetings, as well as a never-to-be-forgotten district conference. During the conference I felt something was missing but was not sure what it was. Finally, I realized that Kelepi was not in attendance. This was the first conference I could ever remember attending in Ha'apai without seeing the thin body and grey, piercing eyes of Kelepi. I looked closer and couldn't see his wife, Suli, either.

When the meeting ended, I asked the district president where Kelepi was. He explained that Kelepi had suffered a stroke and had been totally helpless for many months. His wife and other family members were providing total care for him. I immediately made arrangements to visit him.

As I arrived at Kelepi's house and greeted Suli and several other family members, a flood of memories washed over me. Everything was immaculate and clean, just like Kelepi and Suli would have it. Even though the house was old and worn, it seemed new and fresh from all the marvelous memories I had of it and its occupants.

The family ushered me into the room where Kelepi was lying on several beautiful mats with his head resting on a colorful, hand-embroidered pillow. He was covered with a clean white sheet. Even though he was perfectly motionless and his eyes were closed, it was wonderful to see him again.

He was so quiet, moving so little, that it was hard to tell whether he was even alive. I had always known him to be thin, but now he was barely a wisp. His wife apologized profusely for the fact that Kelepi could not give me a formal welcome to his home. She explained that he had been lying this way for months and didn't recognize anyone. He couldn't speak, but she knew he appreciated her constant care. She explained that lately his eyes were nearly always closed and his breathing was becoming more shallow.

Suli put her cheek on his chest near his heart and said, "It is still warm. I'll check his feet, to know for sure." Some of the older Tongans believed that when a person dies, his spirit comes out through the soles of the feet; thus, if the feet are warm, he is still "there." After checking his feet, she looked up and said, "He is still alive."

Suli sat by her husband's side, took hold of his hand, and spoke to him as though he were fully conscious. "Kelepi, Kolipoki has come to visit us. Our family is here to greet him formally on your behalf. We know you cannot talk or move. We also know that you are still alive. We hope you will accept our welcome to Kolipoki on your behalf."

She then put his hand down and motioned to the other family members to begin the rather formal welcoming ceremony, which included some lengthy speeches. There were tears of gratitude and expressions of deep love and appreciation. When they finished, it was my turn to respond. I asked if it would be all right if I went to Kelepi's side and spoke directly to him. They agreed.

I took his thin hand in mine, looked at his weather-beaten, craggy face, and tried to say something, but my emotions were too strong and I couldn't speak. As I looked at Kelepi, I did not see an old man about ready to die, but a faithful son of God, full of courage, devotion, and enormous strength. To me he looked as strong as when he had acted as "the Lord's wind," rowing a young missionary to shore.

Finally, I squeezed his hand and said, *"Kelepi. Ko au Kolipoki. Malo e tau moe ngaue lahi kuo fai."* (Kelepi. It's me, Elder Groberg. Thank you for all the great work you have accomplished.)

As soon as I said those words, his eyes popped open, his hand squeezed mine, and his lips began to move, even though the rest of his body was perfectly still.

"Ue—Kolipoki—Kuo ke ha'u." (Oh, Elder Groberg, you've finally come.)

He then launched into several minutes of some of the most profound and beautiful words I have ever heard. He spoke loud enough for all in the room to hear.

"Don't thank me. I thank you. Thanks for believing in me and in the Tongan people." He spoke nonstop for about five minutes testifying to his family of the truths of the gospel. He concluded by saying, "You know there is no more important work in all the world than testifying of Jesus. This includes missionary work, temple work, and helping others understand and live the truths of His gospel. That's it, that is what life is for—to learn to know God, to learn to love Him, to obey Him by going to the

Kelepi La'iafe Ikatauimoana Talakai and his wife, Suli.

temple, and to serve Him by serving His children. *"Ofa atu, Kolipoki Nofo a."* (I love you, Elder Groberg. Good-bye.)

Then, as quickly as his words had started, they stopped. His eyes closed, his hand released its grip, and he was exactly as he had been when I arrived. The only sounds or movements in the room were the muffled sobs of joy and the wiping of tears by those present.

I reverently looked at him and replied, "Good-bye, Kelepi. Godspeed in all you do. Good-bye." I sat there for a long time, as did everyone else, trying to comprehend what had been said and felt. No one wanted to move. We all wanted to stay under the beautiful influence of the Spirit of peace and love that was so powerfully present.

After our meeting, I flew back to Nuku'alofa for another conference there, then returned to Hawaii. When I arrived in Honolulu, I was given a telegram that read: "Kelepi La'iafe Ikatauimoana Talakai quietly passed away last night. There were no more words. His feet were cold this morning. Funeral at noon. Suli."

What a legacy of faith Kelepi built and left for his family and all of us. What a difference one man can make. How clearly he discerned between things temporal, which may or may not be important, and things spiritual, which are always important—even vital. As I folded the telegram, I closed my eyes and breathed a final thank you: "*Malo Kelepi. Malo e tau moe ngaue lahi kuo fai. Folau a.*" (Thank you, Kelepi. Thank you for all the great work you have done. Sail on.)

It seemed to find its mark, as I felt a slight rush of acceptance and response. I was more determined than ever to constantly preach the truth, testify of the Savior, and remain faithful to my last breath.

Chapter 12

Return of the Prodigal

Several years after returning from being mission president in Tonga, I was told that an old friend there had gotten into trouble and been excommunicated from the Church. I didn't want to believe it was true, but it was. I wanted to help in any way I could, but wasn't sure how.

I found some quiet time and prayed about this man and his family, wanting to know if there was anything I could do. Into my mind came a discussion we had had years ago when his son turned missionary age. I had always assumed his son would serve a mission, and was surprised to find that his father was insisting that he go to school overseas instead. I couldn't believe it and asked if I could talk to his son. He agreed. His son was obviously conflicted: He wanted to serve a mission, but at the same time he wanted to obey his father. After much prayer, I met with the father and reviewed the fact that his son was of age, had his own moral agency, and had to live with the decisions he made. I pled with him to allow his son to make his own decision. The Spirit touched this father, for he agreed to this.

We called his son in and asked what he truly desired to do. He said he wanted to obey his father, but even more he wanted to obey his Father in heaven. He continued, saying that after much fasting and prayer, he felt he should serve a mission now and see about more schooling later.

His father bowed his head in disappointment and sobbed. His son had always been obedient, and I could tell he was struggling to reconcile his and his son's differing feelings. There was a long period of tense quiet, and then I felt impressed to say to the father that this was the right decision and would prove to be a great blessing to him and his family. I further said that the day would come when he would be eternally grateful for his son's mission. The father eventually raised his head, tried to smile, and said, "I believe what you have said. It is hard, but I will stick with our agreement and my son's decision."

As this memory came to my mind, I wrote a letter to my friend. I told him of my love for him and his family and reminded him of that evening long ago when the decision was made for his son to serve a mission. I reminded him of what a good missionary his son had been, and what a good husband and father and member of the Church he was now. I thanked him for raising such a good son. I expressed my love and confidence in him. I told him that my faith and prayers would be with him and his family forever, and that I would do anything I could to help them. I waited and waited, but received no response.

Sometime later, while I was thinking and praying about what more I might do, the thought came to me to contact this man's son, who had been one of our great missionaries. As we visited, I could tell he was even more concerned than I was. He and his wife and his mother were doing their best to help. They were finding, however, that when someone moves himself into the darkness, it is very difficult and often takes a long time to move back into the light. As difficult as it was for them to watch their father suffer, they understood that ultimately it wasn't up to them. Their father had to find his way back on his own time. I encouraged them to keep trying and assured them of my constant prayers on their behalf.

Years went by. Then, one evening, I had an unusually vivid dream: I found myself in a large city leaving a chapel after a meeting and getting into a taxi to go to the airport. On the way, I felt impressed to tell the driver to turn right on the next street. He was surprised and told me that this turn was not on the way to the airport and, in fact, would take us into a rather dangerous part of town. I insisted that was where I wanted to go, so he grudgingly complied.

He asked for the address of the person I was looking for. I told him I wasn't sure, but we needed to turn left at the next corner. He turned, and we found ourselves facing a dark, dead-end street. This was getting scary, but I still asked him to turn down the next alley. He refused, saying we were in a bad part of town and he felt great danger down that alley. I felt danger also, but a strong feeling we should go there. I assured him that I knew we would be all right, so he hesitatingly turned down the alley.

It was very dark, and every sound made us jump. Suddenly, I sensed a movement behind a large dumpster and got out to see what it was. "You're crazy!" the driver yelled. I agreed, but being driven by a stronger force, I went to see who was there.

As I moved closer, I heard a rattling moan. Something impelled me to call out my friend's name and, as I did, the dark lump sagged into muffled sobs. I peeled the rags from the shaking form, and there was my friend. His tears were slowly washing away the dirt and grime on his unkempt face. I sensed that my tears and the tears of many others were joining with his and in some way helping in this cleansing process.

The driver yelled that we had to get out of there—he could hear new, strange, and ominous noises, so he was leaving with or without me. I looked at the taxi, and then at my friend. His eyes pled, "Don't leave me—don't leave me."

I don't know what happened next, as I awoke with a start and a gasp. I tried to go back, but the dream was gone, as was my sleep. I knew my friend was in serious trouble. What should I do? The dream seemed incongruous, as the dark alley of a big city is far from the open dirt roads and moonlit paths of Tonga. As I prayed for guidance, I felt impressed to call his missionary son again.

When I located him, I found he had recently moved to Dallas, Texas. I told him I thought he should invite his parents to come and visit them. He agreed. I asked him to try extra hard to help his dad, as I was sure he needed it. He said he would do his best. We visited for a long time, recalling many wonderful missionary experiences. As I hung up the phone, I felt at peace, knowing that we had obeyed the prompting of the Spirit so the situation was in far more capable hands than ours.

Not long after this conversation, Elder Thomas S. Monson told me of an experience he had at the Salt Lake City airport. He had returned from a conference late one evening and was on his way to a waiting car when out of the corner of his eye he saw a man standing alone in the baggage claim area. Elder Monson proceeded to the car, but as he reached for the door, he felt impressed to turn around, go back to the baggage area, and say something to that man. He did so, and as he spoke to him he recognized him as my friend, for he had met him on several prior occasions. He gave him a hug and some much-needed encouragement, along with some inspired advice. My friend told him he had just come from Tonga and was on his way to Texas to visit his son and his family for an extended period. Elder Monson bade him farewell, and they went their separate ways.

Many months later I received an assignment to attend a stake conference in Dallas. Included in the packet was a special letter authorizing me to restore the needed blessings to my friend while there.

After the conference, I met in the stake president's office with my friend, his wife, their missionary son, and his wife. The Spirit of the Lord was present in rich, even overflowing abundance as the restoration to all that is good and right and eternal took place. Tears and sobs of love and joy for the fulfillment of years of effort and dreams filled the room. Angels and others were present. The occasion was even more meaningful as everything was done in the beautiful Tongan tongue, which allowed the feelings to go directly to the heart of everyone present. What joy and beauty there is in rescuing souls!

It is impossible to know all who were part of this rescue. Many did a little here and a little there—the wife, the son, friends from both sides of the veil, Elder Monson following the prompting of the Spirit, and countless others who heeded promptings and may not have even known they had helped. But most of all, the Savior had healed the wounds. Not only had He made it all possible, He had been more intimately involved than any of us could imagine. I know He wants all of us to partake of His blessings, including His forgiveness. I know He has paid the price and rejoices when others listen to the promptings of His spirit and help bring souls to Him through faith and repentance.

I looked at those present and saw light and joy in their eyes. I looked beyond them and sensed that same light and joy coming from other spheres. It was beautiful! I asked those present to never cease their efforts to join with the Savior in helping others come to repentance through faith on Him, then continue on to be perfected in Him. I ask the same of myself and everyone, as I know any of us, anytime or anywhere, can find ourselves desperately in need of such help. Likewise, we can be of immeasurable help to those in need if only we will listen and do something. If we sincerely try, we will be blessed in our efforts. Those on the other side never stop helping, and neither should we.

As we concluded our meeting, I sensed the missionary son had something important to say, so I called on him. He stood and said, "I want to read a few verses from the Bible, changing just two words."

He then read the parable of the prodigal son, but when he came to the last verse he read, " . . . for this [my father] was dead, and is alive again; and was lost, and is found" (Luke 15:32). Everyone present (and it was more than the five of us) felt an intense radiation of the Spirit as we were enveloped in an atmosphere of light and goodness and love.

Almost immediately the stake president knocked on the door. I felt as though I was being awakened from a dream. The president said we must leave for the airport or I would miss my flight. We hugged each other again and bade farewell, and I left for the airport with the stake president.

On our way, I noticed a road I thought I had seen before. I started to say, "Turn right at this intersection," but stopped after the first word. The stake president asked, "What did you say?" I responded, "Oh nothing, I was just wondering what is off to the right." He replied, "You don't want to go there—it is a dangerous part of the city." I watched in silent contemplation as I recognized many things I had seen before, including a distant alleyway. The stake president asked if I was all right. "Yes," I smiled, "I'm just fine." We got to the airport on time.

As I flew home, I pondered the importance of praying harder so we can be more effective in helping prodigals return. The prodigal we need to pay the most attention to, and can be the most help to, is our own self. After ourselves come members of our family, then close friends and others. We are all prodigals to some degree, and all need to return to the deepest recesses of the Savior's love. I know there is joy and beauty and comfort there. That is where He wants us to be, and He will help us get there. There are so many prodigals, including ourselves, and there is so much joy in their return, shouldn't we help more by praying harder, working harder, and being more believing?

Years later, I was assigned to a conference in Tonga. After the Sunday session, I met my friend. He was being pushed in a wheelchair by his faithful wife. How I admired them both! As we greeted each other with a Tongan kiss, he whispered, "Everything is fine. I am clean and ready to go. I thank you and everyone who helped. I love my wife. I love my son. I am grateful for his mission. I love my family. I love you. Good-bye."

Shortly after returning home, I received a message that my friend had passed away in full fellowship. Immediately, everything connected with his life came flowing back into my mind. I seemed to see him, then his faithful wife, then his missionary son, then others, mostly his family, smiling with a radiance beyond compare. Behind and above and through them all, I sensed an even deeper, more all-encompassing smile, as though the One who made it all possible was showing His joy in the return of the prodigal. I felt warm all over and resolved to put forth even more effort in this great, joy-filled cause of serving the Lord in helping prodigals return to Him.

Chapter 13

Open Your Eyes!

I received an assignment to hold two stake conferences on succeeding weekends in Lima, Peru. Fortunately, Jean was able to accompany me, and we scheduled youth, missionary, and leadership meetings at various locations during the week between the two conferences. We were excited to return to Peru, as it had been many years since our last visit there. Our flights from Salt Lake went well, and our plane landed in Lima on schedule. But when we pulled up to the gate and prepared to disembark, strange delays began to happen.

First, it took an unusually long time to get the paperwork done before the plane's door opened and we could exit. Then, in the hall to the Immigration checkpoint, one of the doors was locked. The entire group of passengers had another long wait until an officer came and opened the door. By the time we got to Immigration, two other international flights had disembarked, and the lines were very long. We were tired and wondered what else could go wrong. Sure enough, there was another delay as our bags were literally the last ones off the conveyor belt. When we eventually got through Immigration and Customs it was close to midnight.

Finally, with bags in hand, we entered the congested waiting area where, despite the late hour, hundreds of people were milling around—greeting travelers, offering taxis and hotels, or selling various items. We were met by a member of the Area Presidency and his wife who had been patiently waiting for us. Just as we crossed the crowded street and were melding into the throngs of humanity and cars, we heard the plaintive call: *"Kolipoki! Kolipoki!"*

The last thing I thought I would hear in Lima, Peru, at midnight was someone calling my Tongan name! Yet there it was, clearly, *"Kolipoki!"* We turned around in amazement and saw a woman coming up to us, all out of breath from pushing her luggage cart, trying not to lose sight of us. *"Kolipoki, Kolipoki, 'ofa o tokoni mai!"* (Elder Groberg, Elder Groberg, please help me!)

I responded, *"Ue! Koe ha 'oku ke fai i heni?"* (Wow! What are you doing here?) Speaking to her in Tongan calmed her down considerably.

It turned out that a little earlier that evening this faithful Tongan sister had arrived in Lima. She had come to meet her daughter at the conclusion of her mission in Peru. The daughter had made arrangements with the mission president to fly from her last area in Cuzco so as to arrive in Lima about the same time as her mother's plane did. Something went wrong, and mother and daughter had missed each other.

The mother didn't speak any Spanish and precious little English, but finally made it through Immigration and Customs. As she entered the passenger waiting area, she was pressed on every side by the mobs of people. She looked and looked but could not see her daughter. She kept asking where her daughter might be, but no one seemed to understand or even care; they just wanted to sell her something or get her in a taxi. To all these requests she simply said, "No," (works in both English and Spanish) as she knew she must stay there to find her daughter.

She was worried, but with fervent faith she found a small corner, bowed her head, and prayed and prayed and prayed. She knew the Lord would help her. During her prayer she felt a sudden impression like a voice that said, "Open your eyes now!" She obeyed, and lo and behold, passing a little way in front of her she saw Kolipoki! Upon hearing her story, we were able to contact the mission president by cell phone, and before long mother and daughter were safely together and on their way to a missionary apartment.

What are the odds of such a thing happening on its own? There were millions of people in Peru, and probably no more than three or four who could speak Tongan. A faithful Tongan woman arrives in Lima, finds that she has a problem, prays in faith, listens, opens her eyes, and sees someone she knows who speaks Tongan and can help her! Even the greatest of skeptics would likely acknowledge that this was more than a coincidence.

Someone quipped to me: "You thought you were coming to Peru for some stake conferences, but maybe you were really coming to answer the sincere prayer of a faithful Tongan woman." I thought of the many delays we had experienced that evening, and marveled at how the Lord works in ways that are beyond our comprehension. I also realized that after this good woman prayed in faith, she still had to obey and *open her eyes* immediately or she would have missed seeing us. The same is true of all of us. Unless we promptly obey the impressions we receive, we may miss the help available to us or the opportunities for us to help others.

Often the need to give or receive help involves those closest to us. Occasionally, I hear husbands or wives complaining about their spouses or their children. Serious problems may require professional help. But where there is honesty, good will, and a sincere desire to work things out rather than merely complain, the solution is to pray in faith, then open our eyes and see our spouse for who he or she really is—or can become. We need to see our children for who they really are: a source of eternal joy, not a hindrance to it. Regardless of what stage they are in, we must see their potential and lovingly help them move to the next stage.

How we "see" things makes such a difference. For example: A husband once told me he felt that his wife was not really interested in him "because every time we travel for a distance in the car, she immediately falls asleep and ignores me." Someone close by responded, "My wife does the same thing and I feel to say to her: 'Sleep on, my love. I know how hard you work and how tired you must be. How glad I am you can get some rest.'"

Too often we believe the world when it says: "Seeing is believing." I have learned that in reality the reverse is true: "Believing is seeing!" As we pray in faith and listen to spiritual promptings, God will open our eyes and we will be able to "see" things we otherwise may have missed. Often the help we need is passing right in front of us, but we don't open our eyes. Elizabeth Barrett Browning put it well when she wrote: "Earth's crammed with heaven and every common bush afire with God, but only he who sees takes off his shoes."

As I have reviewed past experiences, I have been fascinated by how many times the eyes of my understanding have been newly opened so I could "see" a new dimension, learn a new lesson, or recognize more clearly the Lord's intimate guidance, intervention, and encouragement. I have come to realize that the most significant experiences in life are not necessarily the most spectacular. Some of the seemingly simple experiences have the deepest impact over time.

I have learned that anyone, anywhere, regardless of their calling or station in life, who will humbly pray for God's guidance and then follow the direction received, will have eternally meaningful experiences. They will be able to "see" God's hand in their lives. President Joseph F. Smith wrote: "As I pondered over these things . . . the eyes of my understanding were opened" (Doctrine and Covenants 138:11).

The more humble and obedient we are, the more the Lord can give us the ability to see. When the Savior asked His disciples, "Having eyes, see ye not?" (Mark 8:18), He could have been saying to all of us, "Open your eyes. See who I really am and how much I have done and am doing for you. See who you really are and how much more you are needed to help others. Please follow me. Don't be like the unbelieving of whom I must say, 'their eyes they have closed,' but be believing so I can say, 'but blessed are your eyes, for they see'" (see Matthew 13:15–16). The Savior is always urging us to be more obedient so we can see more clearly—knowing that as we do, we will understand more and have more joy.

God opened the eyes of Elisha and then, at his request, the eyes of his faithful servant (see 2 Kings 6:16–17). He allowed Enoch, Moses, Abraham, Peter, Paul, the brother of Jared, Nephi, Alma, Joseph Smith, Brigham Young, and many, many others to see things that were beyond their mortal comprehension.

How many eyes did the Savior open, both physically and spiritually? How many more will He open as eternity rolls on? God is the great Creator. He is the Giver of life and opportunity and hope. His hand is in all that is around us. I am confident that when we finally see things as they really are, we will bow in even deeper adoration for all the Lord has done for us. It will be so much more than we ever thought, we will want to say, "I had no idea! If only I had known!"

A good Tongan sister in far-off Peru found herself in trouble. She prayed in faith, believing. She heard the Lord's prompting, obeyed, opened her eyes, and received the help she needed in a way we can only call miraculous. It can be the same with us if we will pray, obey, and open our eyes!

Chapter 14

IT WOULD NOT CLOSE

For three years I supervised the work of the Church in Arizona and Nevada and learned to love the people of those great states. One of the several missions I visited regularly was the Arizona Holbrook Mission. It included most of the Native American population in Arizona and the Four Corners area. I was often on the reservations and frequently marveled at the sense of space and beauty typical of that magical land.

During one of my visits to that area I held a meeting with the mission president in Holbrook. He explained how desperately they needed more couple missionaries. In those days, couples called to the Arizona Holbrook Mission brought their own house trailer and were assigned to one of the branches scattered throughout the reservation, where they helped the branch members and supported the young single missionaries in every way they could.

While we were having this discussion, the doorbell rang. There stood a senior sister who had come with her husband to start their mission. We asked where her husband was, and she pointed to the driveway, where a truck pulling a camper was parked. We asked if they would like to come in and have

Navajo hogan.

something to eat and take a little rest before getting their assignment. She replied that it would probably be best if the mission president just gave her the assignment, and they would be on their way.

This seemed a little strange, so I asked if it would be all right for me to speak to her husband in his truck. She suggested it might be best to just leave him alone but, with a shrug of her shoulders, said it was up to me. She and the mission president and his wife went into the mission home and I walked out to the truck. As I got close, I detected a little flurry of activity as the husband quickly rolled down both windows. I introduced myself and we shook hands through the open window. It was obvious from the smell that there had been some recent smoking. I felt impressed to ignore that and thanked him for coming with his wife to serve these wonderful people.

He quickly responded, "Look, this is my wife's mission! We were married in the temple, but I haven't been back since. As you can tell, I still smoke some, but I love my wife. She is a good woman and we have raised a good family. She has always wanted to go on a mission, and we figured this was about her only

Navajo reservation.

chance. I promised her and I promise you, I will support her and help her in any way I can. I love her and have always been loyal to her. Back home she was our Relief Society president, and I always helped her. I am trying to quit my habit, but it is hard. Please give us a chance."

This unexpected response surprised me. I had never been faced with this sort of situation. As I looked at this atypical missionary, my heart melted and I replied, "Not only is she a good woman, but she has a good husband. This mission will be a great blessing to both of you, and you will be a great blessing to many others. Now, in addition to your obvious love and support of your wife, what other skills do you have?" He gave a relieved smile and replied that he had been a mechanic all his life and was handy with electrical and plumbing problems as well.

With the added information on this brother's mechanical skills and abilities, the mission president felt inspired to assign the couple to a particular branch, and he also gave them a special assignment to cover the entire mission in servicing all of the missionary trucks and house trailers. At that time the missionaries lived in house trailers and drove pick-up trucks in order to cover the long distances on often poor roads. The husband accepted that assignment, with the emphatic qualification, "Just as long as you never call on me to speak!" I noticed a deep smile of love and gratitude from his wife.

I met this couple several times over the next two years. At every zone meeting, the husband could be seen happily servicing the missionary trucks, while his wife helped with the music and other parts of the zone meetings. A year later, the mission president told me they had saved more than $50,000 on automotive repairs, compared with the previous year. He attributed the savings to the conscientious work of this missionary.

Nearly a year after that report, we went to a zone meeting in a distant corner of the reservation. I noticed the missionary trucks lined up with their hoods propped open and this good brother going about servicing the trucks with an unusually radiant smile on his face. The mission president mentioned to me that this couple's mission would be completed next month. I greeted the husband, thanked him for his months of hard work, and congratulated him on faithfully fulfilling his mission with his wife. His lips quivered a bit, and I sensed he had something to say, so I asked what it was. Hesitantly he replied, "I'm sort of greasy and dirty, but do you think it would be all right if I came into the zone meeting today? I could finish working on the trucks after the meeting while the missionaries are eating."

"Of course you can." I felt there was something more, so I asked, "And what else?"

"Do you think it would be all right if I said something to the missionaries?"

"You will be our final missionary speaker," I replied. He smiled and wiped his hands, and we went into the chapel, where the assembled missionaries were singing hymns with power and deep feeling.

The zone conference proceeded as outlined, but I perceived a heightened sense of warmth and goodness. Everyone had noticed, especially his wife, that our "mechanic missionary" had come to the zone meeting and was seated on the back row. Everyone was surprised and delighted when we called on him to speak.

Slowly, he walked to the rostrum, with every eye in the room glued on him. He humbly stood, looked out over the missionaries, made contact with his wife's brimming eyes, and began speaking.

"Missionaries, I haven't spoken at meetings much, so I'm not very good. All I want to say is I know you are doing God's work and He is watching over you. As you know, I have asked each companionship to make a list of needed repairs and things to check on their truck, put the list on the front seat, and then prop the hood up. When I complete the repairs and servicing, I check the list, then close the hood, so you will know your truck is safe to go.

"Seven weeks ago at a zone conference, I went down the list on a particular truck, finished the repairs, and went to close the hood, but it would not close! I was a little frustrated, so I made sure the rod was released and pulled down hard, but it still would not close. I kicked the truck and pulled even harder, but it would not close. I had a feeling that maybe I had forgotten something, so I checked the list over and looked at everything to make sure I had completed each item. I had done everything—so I tried again to close the hood, but it would not move.

"I could have become angry and said something I shouldn't have, but instead I said a little prayer for help. I then crawled under the front of the truck and began looking. Suddenly, I noticed that a bolt attaching the steering rod to a front wheel at a critical connecting point had been sheared off and was barely hanging in place. I tapped it once and it fell out. I went to my supplies, got a new bolt, installed it, and came out from under the truck. I checked the list again, went to the hood, and it closed with ease!

"Missionaries, God is aware of you and the work you are doing. He is watching over and protecting you. I know He lives. I know He loves you. I know He loves all of us."

Then, looking straight at his wife he continued, "I haven't touched one for seven weeks, Dear. It's not a problem anymore. As soon as we return home, we're going back to the temple. I love you. I love the missionaries. I love the Lord. I know this is His true Church. In the name of Jesus Christ, amen."

As this remarkable missionary sat down, there was not a dry eye in the room. I sensed that those same emotions reverberated throughout eternity. I realized that great good can be done to and through any of God's children who love purely and serve loyally. This good mechanic received his witness in a way that made sense to him. I marveled at how the Lord knows each of us and speaks to us anytime, anywhere, in the way we can best understand and accept. The fruit of true love and honest service is always sweet.

Chapter 15

THE GIFT OF FORGIVENESS

When we give the gift of forgiveness, great blessings flow to everyone involved. Whenever we decide to do anything good, such as giving the gift of forgiveness, two forces are set in motion. One is from the evil one, trying to get us to fear or delay or not act at all. The other is from the Lord, encouraging us to act positively and quickly on these promptings.

Once at a stake conference in Utah, shortly before Christmas, I felt impressed to talk on the gift of forgiveness, calling it one of the best gifts anyone could give. I spoke of the Savior and how, at this time of year, we celebrate His birth by giving gifts, hopefully in remembrance of the many gifts He gives to us, including the great gift of forgiveness. I explained that I felt there may be some present who had bad feelings toward members of their family. I encouraged them to give the gift of forgiveness and set those feelings right—and to do it now, while the Spirit was influencing them to do so. I remember saying a few other things like, "They will accept your efforts," "You will feel better," "Our Father in Heaven will be pleased," and "We can't be totally pure in heart as long as we have bad feelings toward others." I was sure it was the message the Lord wanted given at that time and place.

Later, a sister from that stake asked if she could visit with me. She said she had grown up in an LDS family with several brothers and sisters who were all active except one brother. This brother was not only inactive but quite belligerent toward his family and the Church. He had not served a mission. He had married out of the Church and moved to a distant state. He had maintained very little contact with his family and none with the Church.

This sister had tried to work with her brother, but he spurned all her efforts as well as those of the rest of the family, especially his parents. Years went by, and their mother and father became ill and passed away. The estranged brother did not attend the funerals. This sister became angry and accused him of being insensitive. She complained bitterly by phone about the "suffering he had caused their parents" and suggested that he had "speeded their demise by the pain he had caused them." She insisted that he change, but to no avail. After the last funeral, all communication between the two ceased.

Now, years later, during that Christmastime stake conference the impression came to her: "Go home and call your brother right now and apologize to him." She resisted that feeling, saying, "*Me* apologize to *him?* He needs to apologize to me and the rest of the family." However, the influence of the Spirit stayed with her, and when the session ended she went directly home and called her brother.

She was sure he would be home, as he had often bragged about Sunday being his TV day. She was scared, but dialed the number anyway. Sure enough, he answered.

"Hello."

"Hello, Bill? This is your sister Mary."

"Oh, Mary, what the ________ do you want?"

"Bill, I've called to ask your forgiveness."

"My forgiveness? For what? What have you done now?"

"Bill, I've had bad feelings toward you for some time. I want to apologize and ask you to forgive me for these bad feelings."

"Aw, c'mon, Mary, what are you really after?"

"Bill, I'm serious. I need your forgiveness for my bad feelings. There's no catch, I'm not asking anything else. Please, Bill, tell me you forgive me!"

"Mary, what's gotten into you? Why is this suddenly so important to you?"

"Well, Bill, I've just come from a conference session where the speaker told us that we can't be totally pure in heart if we have bad feelings toward others. But more than that, you're my brother, and I feel a spirit of love for you and a deep spirit of sorrow for the bad feelings I have had toward you. Please, Bill, it's Christmastime—gift time—please give me this gift of forgiveness. I love you, and I'm sorry for my past feelings. They have changed. Please, can I have your forgiveness?"

There was a long silence. Then a different Bill answered: "Mary, if this means so much to you—of course I forgive you. I don't know what for, but if that's what you want, fine. Now let me ask *you* something."

"Oh, thank you, thank you, Bill. Thanks for your forgiveness. I feel so much better. What did you want?"

"Mary, could we start talking more? Lately I have been missing our family and have even been thinking a little about the Church."

Totally surprised, Mary responded, "Of course. I'd love to visit more."

By now there were tears of love and gratitude on both ends of that telephone call. It may seem silly to pay long-distance charges just to hear one another cry—but it was worth it!

Mary explained that she was not expecting her brother to say anything about restoring family ties or returning to the Church. That was not her motivation. She had no outside agenda. She simply wanted to purify her heart and sincerely ask for forgiveness for her former bad feelings. She knew that her brother had his own moral agency, and she would leave the rest to him and the Lord.

As she told her story, I felt more strongly than ever that *anyone, anywhere, anytime* can give and receive the gift of forgiveness. We need only to have faith enough to take the step. When our hearts are pure, or on the way to becoming pure, it is amazing how much better things go for everyone.

Over the next few years Bill strengthened his ties with his siblings and the Church. Eventually his wife and children joined the Church. Yes, the gift of forgiveness—the gift of love—the gift of testimony—all these continue giving forever.

Chapter 16

Comfort My Soul

When things are going well, we often assume they will continue that way, but seldom is that the case. Sometimes storms come with little or no warning—no one is immune. When we find ourselves in the midst of a storm, if we will deepen our trust and strengthen our faith in the Lord, He will comfort our souls and help us through.

In 1977, about a year after our family moved to Hawaii, where I had been assigned as Area Supervisor for the Church, a political proposal with deep moral ramifications arose. Public hearings were held, and many Church members as individuals attended and expressed their feelings, which were mostly against the proposal. Some people must have assumed that the members spoke under my direction, for soon I began receiving threatening phone calls and letters. I suppose those people felt that if they could make life miserable enough for me and my family, we would try to influence local Church members to change their position. It was a tense and trying time for us, but since there was no physical violence, only verbal abuse and general threats, we continued our everyday pattern. We didn't tell the children, as we didn't want to frighten them.

John and Jean and family in Hawaii.

The threats became more and more serious. Then one day I received a letter at my office containing kidnapping threats. I contacted our local Church attorney, who had an idea of who might be behind this. Contacts were made through some intermediaries, and almost immediately the threats stopped. We were greatly relieved and assumed that this nonsense was over.

October general conference was approaching, and I had been assigned to speak. Jean was expecting our eleventh child on November 10, but wanted to support me at the conference. She asked her doctor if she could travel with me, and he gave her a letter of permission, on the condition that she be back in Hawaii by October 10. We found a wonderful young couple to stay with our children and left for conference with calm hearts. While in Salt Lake City we checked regularly with the children and the couple, who reported that all was well. Little did we suspect that this was the proverbial calm before the storm.

We scheduled our return to Hawaii through Seattle so we could visit our teenage daughter who was staying with my sister for a while. To comply with the doctor's deadline, we booked a flight to leave Seattle Monday morning, October 10.

Sunday evening, October 9, we were enjoying a pleasant visit with our daughter and my sister and her family, when suddenly it became obvious that the baby was determined to arrive early. We needed a doctor but didn't know where to turn. My sister and her husband had two fine adopted sons, but had not been able to have children naturally, so they did not have such a doctor. The ward Relief Society president gave us the name of a doctor she felt was the best in the area. She told us that he was extremely busy, so if we could not get through to him (which we couldn't) we should go directly to Valley General Hospital in nearby Renton and ask for help.

My brother-in-law and I gave Jean a blessing, then drove to the hospital, arriving late that night. We explained to the helpful receptionist that Jean was about to have a baby, but since we were just passing through we did not have a doctor. I assured her that our insurance was reliable. She believed me, made some phone calls, and soon informed us that there was a doctor at the hospital waiting to assist with another delivery, and he was willing to stay and help us. "You are very fortunate," she exclaimed. "He is the best doctor in the valley and has a two-year waiting list for new patients." When she mentioned his name, we recognized he was the same doctor the Relief Society president had recommended!

During the long labor some serious complications developed. We were grateful to be in a good hospital with helpful staff, sophisticated equipment, and the special skill and kindness of a wonderful doctor who stayed all night and far into the next day to help strangers in need.

As the hours wore on I had time to visit with the doctor about many things. He was interested in what we were doing and why we were there, which opened the door to a discussion of several important gospel topics. I liked him and felt impressed to mention that my sister had not been able to have children. He was a fertility specialist and agreed to see her as a patient without the two-year waiting time.

For many hours the doctor carefully guided Jean and the nurses through a number of tense situations. I remember, at times when things were most critical, saying in my heart (and sometimes out loud) to Jean and the struggling infant: "Come on—you can make it. I know it's hard, but you can do it. Don't give up; keep trying. You can make it—come on—keep your heart beating—keep coming—you'll be just fine." Little did I know how much or how soon I would need the comfort of those same words.

We were anxious but buoyed up by our deep confidence in God. We felt we were doing all we could, so we could leave the rest to God, knowing He would do what was best. Answers to prayers and priesthood blessings come in many ways, including the enhanced ability of a good doctor.

A calming peace descended and enabled the doctor and Jean and the struggling infant to do their parts. After a difficult fourteen hours, a perfect little girl made her entrance into mortality. What joy! What fulfillment! She was a month early, but healthy, happy, and obviously anxious to be here. We noted the time of birth (12:55 P.M.) and realized that the flight we were booked on was at that moment halfway between Seattle and Honolulu.

As soon as we saw the baby, we knew she was as precious and beautiful as "flowers from heaven" (which in Hawaiian is "leilani"), so we gave her the name of Emily Leilani. While Jean finally got some well-deserved rest, I found a phone and called our children in Hawaii to announce the happy news. They were overjoyed to have a new little sister. I could tell, however, that something was wrong.

Soon the frantic voices of the young couple came on the line. The threats had started again! The couple was terrified and didn't know what to do. The threats were directed at the grade-school children. The young wife was almost beside herself with fear. I wanted to help them but didn't know how.

Suddenly, a memory came to mind of a family home evening we had held shortly after moving into our home in Hawaii. I had blessed and dedicated our home, as we have done wherever we have lived. I distinctly remembered blessing the entire home, including the yard, against the power of evil.

At the time I wondered why I felt impressed to use those words, as everything was so peaceful. Now, listening to this couple's frantic pleas, one of the reasons became clear to me. Without hesitation I said, "Keep the children home from school until we return. As long as they stay in the house or yard, no harm will come to them. I promise. Don't worry. I know everyone will be safe if you do this." How grateful I was for that memory so I could make that promise with certainty. It calmed them (and me) considerably. I hung up the phone feeling that somehow things would be all right, although I did feel sorry for the young couple. What a terrible weight of responsibility had been thrust upon them, as well as the rest of us.

I returned to see how Jean was doing and found her awake. I told her how excited the children were about their new little sister and reported that they were all in good health. Jean, as usual, was a radiant angel, and my heart melted as I saw her cuddling our blessed little bundle of joy. I didn't tell her right then of the seriousness of the situation at home, as I felt she had been through enough.

I stayed with Jean until she was able to rest again, then found a secluded place where I poured out my heart to God. I was so full of gratitude and joy and amazement at the miracle of birth, the wonder of a faithful, loving wife, and the beauty of our lovely daughter, that I could not even think of complaining. From the depths of my soul, I tried to express my gratitude for His blessings and promises. I knew that God understood our situation far better than I did, but I also felt it would be all right to talk to Him about the problems in Hawaii, if for no other reason than to hear myself define them. I started by saying, "I know there is a way out of this, but I don't know what it is. I don't know how long it will be before Jean and the baby can travel. I need to be here to help them, yet I need to be with our other children in Hawaii. I know as long as the children stay home they will be safe, but I'm not sure how much longer the young couple can handle the pressure, or how long the children can stay cooped up in the home and yard. What should I do?"

There was no specific answer, but I felt a peaceful assurance that we would all learn some valuable lessons from this experience, and that everything would turn out all right. I sensed that for now, all we could do was be patient and believing.

Over the next few hours, various impressions came to me, and I made several phone calls. I called my parents, who were surprised and happy with the news of the new baby. I called Jean's parents, who were equally thrilled. As I visited with them, I felt impressed to explain the situation and ask if they could fly to Seattle and return with us to Hawaii. I knew they would be of great comfort and assistance to Jean and the children, as well as to me. They said they would drop everything and come and help.

The next day I felt impressed to call Church headquarters and tell them about our new baby. I called the member of the Quorum of the Twelve who was my first contact. He was out of town, so the secretary transferred me to President N. Eldon Tanner. He was kind and gracious and congratulatory. I felt warm and loved. I decided to mention the problem we were having with the threats in Hawaii. When he heard this he immediately took action, and before the day was over he had a man experienced in security protection on his way to Hawaii. He soon had things under pretty good control. By now the novelty of missing school had worn off and the children kept asking, "Why can't we go to school? Why do we have to stay in our house and yard? I have plans to do things with my friends, why can't I?"

Jean and the baby continued to do well. Her parents arrived in Seattle on Thursday, and on Friday morning, four days after our originally scheduled flight, we gathered up our new little "heavenly lei" and flew back to Hawaii. The children were excited and thrilled with their new sister and the visit from Grandma and Grandpa Sabin. The frightened young couple was anxious to leave their "battle station" and return home. I assured them they would be blessed for their faithfulness under pressure.

I don't know all the details of the security operation, except that contacts were made, action was taken, agreements were reached, and the problems ceased—this time for good. Gradually the security guards, phone monitoring, and other controls were phased out, the children returned to school, and life slowly returned to normal. It was wonderful to be together with Grandma and Grandpa Sabin and not feel the oppressive weight of threats.

Why did this happen? I don't know, and I suppose it doesn't really matter. The important thing is, I relearned that God will comfort our souls in the storms of life. The greater the good we set out to accomplish, the greater the opposition. Having a family and teaching them properly is of the greatest eternal value. Thus, we can expect great trials, as well as great joys, in our families. This should not surprise us. Satan wants to claim our souls and those of our children. He wants our marriages and our families to fail. He wants darkness to reign. Despite this, we needn't worry or back away from our duty to our family (present or future), our community, or others, for God will always support and bless us in our honest efforts to do His will. He wants us to succeed more than Satan wants us to fail—and God is always more powerful.

We related well to the time Alma took a group of missionaries to the apostate Zoramites who had strayed far from the gospel. He sensed an impending storm and prayed fervently for his missionaries: "O Lord, . . . wilt thou comfort their souls in Christ. Wilt thou grant unto them that they may have strength, that they may bear their afflictions which shall come upon them because of the iniquities of this people" (Alma 31:32–33).

Alma's little band of missionaries was given "strength, that they should suffer no manner of afflictions, save it were swallowed up in the joy of Christ" (Alma 31:38). We too have been promised strength to bear all things. As we embark on performing any assignment from God, He will bless and protect us. He will comfort our souls and see us through the storms.

The Savior meekly and patiently overcame the deepest depths of darkness. I sometimes wonder how the forces of evil felt when the Savior refused to give in to pain, intimidation, betrayal, jeering, temptation, dishonesty, or the most exquisite suffering that ever has or ever will be experienced by anyone. They must have been frustrated as they were forced to flee the blinding light of His goodness. What a lesson we should learn from Him! He truly is our Savior and exemplar in all things. I know He will support us in all our trials and troubles as we keep trying and keep believing (see Alma 36:27). No amount of opposition or affliction is so great that it cannot be swallowed up in Christ, for He has already overcome it all and is always there to comfort our souls.

No one is immune from the challenges of life, but even more certainly, no one is outside the reach of the Savior's comforting and saving power!

* * *

Normally, the story would end here, but there is a little more. When everything settled down, Jean's parents returned to Utah. A few months later, her father suddenly became very ill and passed away quickly and unexpectedly. How grateful we were to have had those wonderful weeks with him and Jean's mother in Hawaii! Then, a little over a year after Emily Leilani's birth, my sister gave birth to a healthy baby boy. God is good.

Chapter 17

THE MASTER ARTIST

In many ways the Lord is like a master painter. His works are masterpieces—many still in the making. Sometimes I look at one of His unfinished canvases and cannot understand it. Indeed, the canvas of life often looks like a jumble of what might be called "modern art"—bright colors and strange lines seemingly scattered randomly here and there. Occasionally I find myself wondering why the Painter used that vivid color here, or drew that thin line over there. Then, just when the painting seems most senseless, He draws a single line here, adds a new color there, and presto—it all comes into focus. I finally see why that crisp curve, that dark dot, or that seemingly meaningless mixture of colors were necessary to make the picture complete and beautiful.

One reason why it is so hard to see the big picture of eternity is because in mortality, things are always changing! For example, when we moved from Hawaii to our new home in Bountiful, Utah, all eleven children were at home, at least for the summer. Our first daughter had been attending BYU. Our second daughter soon followed, then our third, and fourth, and so on as the years rolled by.

Then the inevitable happened! First one daughter, then another and another brought special boys home. Each young man nervously asked for a daughter's hand in marriage. We had known it would happen, but it still seemed strange. We had been together for so long, and the older girls were such great helpers—how could we get along without them?

Of course we were happy, as each young man was a returned missionary and each couple had stars in their eyes, love in their hearts, courage in their countenances, and goodness and testimony in their souls. I was privileged to perform each marriage in the temple. Even so, it was difficult to "let go" of our daughters.

Within a few years we were down to seven unmarried children at home, and two of them were attending BYU. That is when we received a call to move to Buenos Aires, Argentina, and serve in the South America South Area Presidency, which at that time covered the countries of Argentina, Chile, Paraguay, and Uruguay.

Jean and I happily accepted this new assignment even though none of our family spoke Spanish. We were told that our apartment in Buenos Aires would be a bit crowded for a family our size. We said that was not a problem, as we were used to doubling up. The Lord had spoken through His leaders, and we knew everything would be fine.

We wondered how to tell the children about the major change coming in their lives. We borrowed a friend's condo in Park City for a special "family overnight." The children could tell that something was in the wind. We introduced the subject by bearing testimony of the rightness of following God's servants, then played a recording of the beautiful song "Don't Cry for Me, Argentina." There were smiles, tears, disbelief, and excitement all mixed together, as animated talking and questioning continued through much of the night.

The Groberg family at the MTC, 1987.

This would be a big step out of our comfort zone for our family. None of us spoke Spanish. The children were pretty entrenched in life in Bountiful; it would be a huge uprooting for them. But when the Lord invites us through His servants to participate in His work, He will help us understand why and how He is painting the canvas in this way.

As we knew they would, things did work out. Two of our children, Gayle and John Enoch, submitted missionary papers and went into the Missionary Training Center in June; the rest of our family followed them a few weeks later to get some special tutoring in Spanish before leaving for South America.

As predicted, we were very tight on sleeping space in Argentina, so our son Tom slept one floor above us in the apartment of Elder and Sister Aldin Porter, who were also serving in the Area Presidency. A year later, our daughter Susan graduated from high school in Buenos Aires and was called on a mission to Uruguay. I had forgotten, but Jean reminded me that when we had gone to Tonga for me to serve as mission president, our daughter Gayle was just a few weeks old. John Enoch was born during our mission there, and Susan was born just a few months after we returned home. We had called these three our "mission babies." Now, for several months, those same three were all serving simultaneously as full-time missionaries. What fulfillment!

As we were nearing the end of three years in Argentina, we felt some strong indicators, both from our own feelings and from statements by those in authority, that we would be staying for at least another year. We loved the people of South America, as well as the Spanish language, and felt we were becoming fairly effective in our work there. Then one day, quite unexpectedly, we received a phone call from Salt Lake City telling us that we were to return to headquarters and supervise the work of the Church in California and Hawaii. Although it was hard to leave Argentina, we were grateful for our new assignment and realized we could continue our association with Latins and Polynesians living in our new area of responsibility.

It is amazing how often change comes along just when we are feeling comfortable where we are. We think we're beginning to understand the painting, and suddenly the Lord introduces a whole new color or shape! I have learned that we must enjoy every minute of every assignment by putting our whole heart and soul into it from the beginning, for we never know when that particular opportunity will be taken away and a new one put in its place. If we haven't given everything in whatever our calling is, we will have missed something we could otherwise have enjoyed.

We never complained, but there was a brief time when we wondered about some of the feelings we had had. The children were the least eager to move, as the Spanish culture and language had become very ingrained in them and they had developed many close friendships. We discussed our feelings and realized anew what a blessing it is to have a prophet who acts according to God's will. What comfort it is to know that doing what he asks will always prove to be right and bring the greatest blessings!

I remembered a stake conference where I was assigned to call a new stake presidency. After the conference a man and his wife asked to speak with me. They had recently been to the temple and felt quite strongly, especially the wife, that the husband would be the new stake president. They were a wonderful, active, fully worthy couple, and they just wondered why they had had these feelings and yet he wasn't called. I explained that the feelings they had received were God's way of letting them know that He knew the husband was worthy to be a stake president. It didn't matter whether the call came or not, but it did matter a great deal that he was worthy—and that was what the Lord was letting them know. I explained that there are many other factors to be considered and that the final call comes through inspiration to the Lord's servants who have been given that specific assignment. This calmed them and answered any lingering questions they had. As I recalled this experience, it also answered any questions our family might have had about our new assignment.

As we prepared to leave Argentina, we related on a personal level to the feelings generated by our theme song. It is easy to say, or sing, "Don't Cry for Me, Argentina"—but it is much harder to

Some friends who came to say farewell to our children at the Buenos Aires airport.

not cry over leaving Argentina. Many of our children's friends rented a bus to come to the airport to bid them farewell. The center of the main waiting area was filled with our children and their friends. When we finally had to break up the circle and pull our children away to get them through Immigration before the plane left, there was literally a small pool of tears left on the cement floor. We shed many, many more tears when we left from Argentina than when we left for Argentina.

We have never left anywhere but what we would like to have stayed longer. Whenever and wherever we put our whole heart and soul into the work of the Lord, we become deeply attached and our lives and emotions become intertwined with those with whom we work. Great love follows in natural course. In fact, the pain we feel at separation is probably a good indicator of how deeply we love those we are separated from.

Thank goodness for the Lord's sacrifice, resurrection, and sealing authority, as well as His ability and willingness to set everything right. Even when (sometimes *especially* when) our mortal circumstances are painful or uncomfortable, He is working diligently to create a masterpiece in us!

I was reminded of this principle years later when a chain of events took me far outside my circle of experience and comfort. It all began when I was "encouraged" by some Church leaders to write a book about my experiences as a young missionary in Tonga. I had written articles and talks before, but writing an entire book was a new experience—one much more difficult than I had anticipated. It took a long time and huge amounts of effort on my part and on the part of many others. When I finally got the manuscript finished and submitted, I breathed a sigh of relief. That sigh, however, was an unexpectedly short one.

When the book was ready to be published, a Church leader who had reviewed the manuscript asked me about some of my experiences in Tonga that had not been included. I said that those particular events had occurred when I was serving as a mission president and not as a young missionary. He then encouraged me to write another book that included my experiences as a mission president in Tonga.

Life is often that way. We complete a major climb to the top of a large mountain and sit to rest and contemplate our "victory." Then we look up and see that there are mountains upon mountains and that, in fact, our climb has just begun. What we have already done is but a preparation for that which we still have to do. We never rest for long.

Even though I was reluctant to write the two books (*In the Eye of the Storm,* published in 1993, and *The Fire of Faith,* published in 1996), I have been grateful for the experience. As the years have passed, I have received hundreds and hundreds of letters, cards, phone calls, and visits from people who say they have been helped in many ways by what they have read in these books. At first I thought that they were just being nice, but eventually it sank in that these writings truly were a source of help to some in need. I have kept some of those letters and notes, and I sometimes wonder what would have happened had I given in to my first inclination to decline the invitation to write the books. At the time I felt that I was too busy to add another project, but because I respected and trusted those who encouraged me to do it, I moved ahead. It was much harder than I had anticipated, and many times I would have stopped, were it not for the assurance that those encouraging me did so because they loved me and wanted the best for me. I sensed that they saw and knew things that at the time I could not see. Their view of the canvas was clearer than mine.

As I stop and contemplate these things, I sense the larger picture—God encourages us to do that which He knows will be best for us and will be the best help to others. If we say that we are too busy, that we do not feel like doing it, or that it is too difficult, He will not force us, but we will never know the joy that comes from doing what He asked. As we climb our own personal mountains, overcome our individual fears, move forward with faith, and simply do what those in authority ask us to do, great blessings and deep satisfaction follow.

But the picture was not yet complete! Some time later, a group with Hollywood connections approached us about the possibility of making *In the Eye of the Storm* into a movie. I was overwhelmed with what it might entail, especially the public attention it might focus on my family. After much prayer and consultation with Church leaders, we determined to allow the film to be done, again in faith that lives could thereby be touched. More than two years later, *The Other Side of Heaven* was released in theaters.

Of the many heartfelt and even miraculous stories that have been shared with me, I would like to tell one that represents the far-reaching effects of this movie. The film has been shown extensively on television, and its coverage has been particularly widespread in Asia and the Muslim world. One mission president reported that they had been having troubles with visas in a particular country. Everything was legal, but the immigration officials constantly harassed the missionaries and turned them back on the slightest technical inconsistency.

One day a group of four missionaries arrived in that country with valid visas, but the immigration personnel found some technicality and pulled them aside. It was their intention to send them back to the country they had come from. They selected one missionary, took him to the office of the "big boss" upstairs, shut the door, and began the interrogation. The missionary did his best to answer the questions fired at him by the official. Suddenly the boss looked at the missionary and said, "Your passport says you are Australian and you talk like an Australian, but you don't look like one."

"That is because I was born in Tonga. My parents moved to Australia when I was very young," explained the nervous missionary.

"Tonga?" replied the man. "Tonga! Last night on TV I saw a movie called *The Other Side of Heaven*. It took place in Tonga. Do you know who Kolipoki is?"

"Yes," smiled the missionary. "My parents knew him well and have told me all about him." There followed a twenty-minute discussion regarding the movie, Tonga, why Mormons go on missions, and a variety of associated topics.

Finally the boss took the missionary downstairs and, with his arm around him, told the other immigration workers, "Everything seems to be in order. Why are you detaining those other three? Let them all pass through and be quick about it!"

One never knows what means God may use to further His work. I am grateful for the encouragement, even the prodding, I received years earlier to write the original book and for the positive feelings to cooperate with those who wanted to make it into a movie. I often wonder what would have happened had I made the choice to stay in my comfort zone and not venture into the writing field.

Yes, the Lord, the Master Painter, knows what He is doing. From His perfect plan of happiness through this mortal existence and into the realms of the eternities, He sees the whole picture. He knows us and loves us beyond measure. As we trust in Him and lean not unto our own understanding, He will direct our paths, and all things shall come together for our good (see Proverbs 3:5–6). We will then be amazed as we look at the nearly finished painting and see how all the lines, colors, tones, and shapes are exactly where they should be. Everything blends into a perfect, beautiful, and, by His grace, celestial picture.

Chapter 18

The Bus Ride

When we moved to Buenos Aires, Argentina, I was amazed at how quickly everyone in the family seemed to adjust to the new culture and different pace. The children were soon speaking fluent Spanish. The language was more of a challenge for Jean and me, but we could at least get along. We soon felt comfortable with the schools, stores, buses, trains, subways, and other everyday aspects of big city life. Maybe we were a little *too* comfortable.

The children often stayed after school for sports or other activities. On those days they would come home on public bus #168, which stopped just a couple of blocks from our apartment. On one such evening, our daughters Jennie, age fifteen, and Viki, thirteen, found the bus very crowded and got separated: Viki was pushed to the front and Jennie to the back of the bus. Jennie noticed that Viki finally got a seat up front, but she then lost track of her through the press of people.

After many stops, the bus finally arrived at our stop. Jennie got off from the rear of the bus and waited for Viki to exit from the front. Many people got off, but she could not see Viki. The doors closed and the bus continued its route. In a panic, Jennie ran after the bus to the next stop, and the one beyond that. Still no Viki! The bus quickly got too far away for Jennie to keep up. She checked along the crowded street everywhere she could think of—but *no Viki*. Frantically Jennie ran home and told us what had happened.

We thought perhaps Viki had gotten off earlier to go to a friend's home and would surely call or be home in a few minutes. But as the minutes ticked by with no calls and no Viki, we became very concerned. It was winter, and the days were short and cool. Buenos Aires is a large city. What do you do when you have a daughter lost in a big city and it is cold and dark? You pray to God and ask friends to help.

Within minutes wonderful friends were making phone calls, checking bus schedules and routes, and doing all they could to locate Viki. We learned that bus #168's route terminated in one of the seamiest sections of town. The bus officials tried to help, but at that time there were no cell phones or other ways of communicating with the drivers until they reached the end of their line. Our concerned friends organized themselves to follow the bus route and check every stop. One car would go directly to the end of the line, even though it was in a scary area. It was still rush

Bus #168.

hour, and the streets were packed with cars, buses, taxis, and mobs of people. Despite this, these loyal friends were ready to do whatever they could to find Viki and return her to us.

As time moved on, desperation began to rear its frightening head. It was hard to not panic. Stories of lost children who never came home flashed through my mind. Our prayers became more intense, our emotions more fragile, and our concern more real. I remember praying: "Oh, Father, please bless Viki—please touch someone, somewhere, to do something to bring her safely home."

It had now been over an hour since Jennie first sounded the alarm. Our friends with cars were just leaving for their agreed-upon areas when a taxi drove up and out popped Viki, asking for money to pay the driver. What a relief—what a blessing—what a miracle! After the fare was paid, everyone gathered around to find out what had happened.

It turned out that when Viki got the seat near the front of the bus she promptly fell asleep and slumped down so that Jennie could not see her from the back of the bus. Being asleep, Viki was unaware when the bus reached her stop. She continued sleeping soundly as the bus drove deeper and deeper into that dangerous part of the city. A kind woman sitting next to her became concerned about this young foreign girl, woke her up, and asked where she was getting off. Fortunately Viki spoke good Spanish and explained where she was supposed to have disembarked. The woman got off at the next stop and took Viki with her. She called a taxi and instructed the driver to take Viki straight to her home (which by then was a long distance away). What gratitude we felt for this unknown woman and the honest taxi driver who brought Viki safely back!

After our nerves had calmed from this unwelcome scare, we all knelt in prayer and thanked God for hearing and answering our prayers. During the prayer I had a brief moment of realization. I had asked God to touch someone, somewhere to do

Viki and Jennie and friends.

something to help Viki get home safely. A woman on the bus responded, woke Viki, put her in a cab, and instructed the driver to bring her safely home. I do not know who the woman on the bus was, and I barely saw the cab driver's hand, but a loving Father in heaven knew them both, called on them to help, and smiled His approval as they responded.

As we listen more attentively to those quiet promptings, we can be that someone, somewhere, helping someone in need. When we come home from a busy day, we check our messages or mail, wanting to know who is trying to contact us and how we should respond. Do we sometimes miss our "spiritual messages" because we do not listen with a purer heart and a more willing attitude? How well we listen to such messages—and how well we respond to them by actually doing something to help—is, in the eternal sense of things, how we express our love to God.

Opportunities to help are all around us. If we don't recognize them, is it because we are not listening well enough? Maybe we are too preoccupied with our own concerns or too busy following our own agenda to hear or feel what others need. Do we let our lives and thoughts get so cumbered with selfishness or sin that we get "past feeling," as Nephi said of Laman and Lemuel? (see 1 Nephi 17:45).

Of the total amount of good done by people, the overwhelming majority consists of small, everyday courtesies and helps. Often the simple decisions—to smile, to say hello, to wish someone well, or to wake a young girl on a bus, put her in a taxi, and send her safely home—can and do make a huge difference in the lives of others.

Think of what a vastly improved place the world would be if all of us made those seemingly little decisions to help rather than hurt, forgive rather than carry a grudge, visit rather than ignore, smile rather than frown, listen rather than tell, and see rather than close our eyes to another's point of view. Whether in Argentina or Asia, Tonga or Idaho, Samaria or Jerusalem, I know the whole universe is full of opportunities to help others *anytime, anywhere,* if only we are willing to listen and act.

Chapter 19

Treasures

While our family was living in Buenos Aires, I received an assignment to tour the Paraguay Asuncion Mission. Mission tours are a good opportunity to meet all the missionaries and many of the investigators and members. When I called the mission president to make the arrangements, he asked if I would like to visit a group of relatively new members from the Chulupi tribe of Nivacle Indians living in a remote area called Mistolar. He said it was difficult to get there and we would have to stay overnight in very primitive conditions, but he knew these faithful members—descendants of Father Lehi—would be thrilled to have us visit them. The purpose of my visit was to meet with and strengthen the missionaries and the members, so I agreed to go. I have been eternally grateful for that experience.

After meeting with the missionaries throughout the main centers of Paraguay, we headed to Mistolar in two heavy-duty Jeeps. It was a trek through a large, swampy jungle area with no real roads in places—not even trails. The first part of the drive was uneventful, but as we got deeper into the swamp, I realized why we needed the four-wheel-drive capability and the winches on both vehicles. Time after time one or the other vehicle would get stuck so deeply that we had to wrap a long steel cable around a big tree nearby to winch it out. There was an abundance of slithery, crawling swamp creatures, and we had to be careful where we stepped when we got out and pushed the vehicles as they slowly inched forward. Fortunately the two vehicles never got stuck at the same time!

Finally, just as the sun was sinking, we pulled into a small native village on the edge of a steep ravine with a rushing river at the bottom. We were warmly greeted by the members. Their excitement at our visit was obvious as they served us a meal and prepared for a special meeting. The branch president explained that years ago some members of the tribe had gone to larger towns seeking employment. There they had met the missionaries, been taught the gospel, and joined the Church. They were truly converted and quickly spread the good news to their families and friends back home. Over the years many missionaries went to Mistolar. They taught and baptized what soon became several hundred members. Many from the second generation were with us now.

Jeep in the mud on the way to Mistolar.

The natives from the village of Mistolar.

Daylight faded and, as there was no electricity, we relied on fires, lanterns, and the few flashlights we had to provide light. The bright eyes of the children literally danced as the flames of the fire shifted back and forth. After the meal we held a meeting in a small community hall packed with members and a few curious investigators. Everything was translated into three languages—Nivacle, Spanish, and English.

To see and hear these modestly dressed natives sing, smile, and testify was heartwarming. I felt their deep sincerity and received spiritual assurance that God was pleased that these humble people were now members of His Church and kingdom. They have a long way to go, as do we all, but they had started the journey.

The members did the best they could to provide sleeping quarters for us, but the mosquitoes and other insects were so numerous that we ended up sleeping in the vehicles. The whole setting reminded me of many similar experiences in Tonga (except we didn't have vehicles for refuge then).

The next morning we met again, gave additional instructions, and shared testimonies. The gratitude of the Saints from Mistolar showed no bounds. Joy leapt from their happy faces. Even though getting there and being there was physically strenuous, the warmth of their love, faith, and appreciation filled our souls such that we didn't mind the mirings, breakdowns, flat tire, broken winch, and myriads of insect bites on the way home.

Those beautiful, faithful people had captured my heart, and I asked the mission president to pray extra hard to find ways to help them both physically and spiritually. As he prayed, he felt impressed to contact the Bureau of Native Affairs. After months of effort, a parcel of land became available that was close to roads and markets yet near enough to Mistolar to allow easy interchange. This land offered a way for the members to improve their circumstances. It was difficult to get through all the red tape of government and other bureaucracies, but eventually everything worked out. Many of these faithful members were able to get parcels of land sufficient to provide for their families. They were anxious to learn to plant, nurture, and harvest crops, as well as tend domesticated animals. They named the place "La Abundancia," or "Bountiful."

A year later, the mission president from Paraguay called and said there were four families from Mistolar ready to be sealed in the temple. Arrangements were made for these children of Lehi to come to the Buenos Aires Temple, which was more than 2,100 kilometers (nearly 1,400 miles) from Mistolar. You can imagine the challenges inherent in this long and difficult journey. They were not sure when they would arrive.

Meanwhile, life moved on for our family in Buenos Aires. One of the advantages of living in that large city was the opportunity to attend various cultural events. One such activity was viewing a traveling exhibit entitled "The Treasures of the Tsars." What a display of opulence we saw in that elaborate array of gowns, cloaks, guns, swords, and jewelry! Even simple household items were heavily gilded with precious metals and decorated with gems. It was obvious that all these items had been spectacularly beautiful when they were created, for even today a glimmer of that original beauty shone through.

The exhibit represented the best that money and power could create in its day, but what we saw now were mostly faded, limp, worn, moth-eaten, molded, tarnished, dulled, or rusted items of little use and hollow worth. As we imagined the original magnificence of the finery of Tsarist Russia, we couldn't help wondering: What was the cost to the multitudes who lived in poverty then?

The next day we took our daughter Susan to the Buenos Aires Temple to receive her endowments prior to serving her mission in Uruguay. What a contrast from the museum the day before! What everlasting treasures we found in the temple!

When we arrived at the temple, we learned that the Saints from Mistolar were there. Coincidence? I don't think so. In addition to the joy of being with our daughter in the temple, we were able to be with the families from Mistolar as they were sealed. What faith and love and gratitude radiated from their faces when they finished that sacred work! They had accepted the knowledge, made the sacrifices, and now received the promised blessings. They knew they could be together forever as families.

Jean and Sue at the Buenos Aires Temple.

They again expressed deep appreciation for our visit to their hard-to-reach location in Mistolar and for our being in the temple with them as they were sealed. I watched the bright eyes of the children and remembered how those same eyes had danced so beautifully before the shifting flames in Mistolar. I thought of the Savior with the children as recorded in Third Nephi, and felt that the radiance in their faces must have been similar. Little did we, or they, know what trials lay ahead of them.

As we drove home from the temple, we couldn't help but compare the "Treasures of the Tsars" with the "Treasures of the Temple." When we left the display in the museum, we felt a little depressed, knowing that the luster of all that finery would continue to deteriorate and dim under the inevitable processes of this earth. By contrast, when we left the temple, we felt buoyed up, knowing that the luster of our missionary daughter and the families from Mistolar would continue to increase in brightness under the inevitable processes of God's eternal laws.

We recalled the Savior's admonition: "Lay not up for yourselves treasures upon earth, where moth and rust doth corrupt, and where thieves break through and steal: but lay up for yourselves treasures in heaven, where neither moth nor rust doth corrupt, and where thieves do not break through nor steal: For where your treasure is, there will your heart be also" (Matthew 6:19–21).

We later learned that on the way back to Mistolar, one of those bright-eyed children became very ill. Shortly after his family arrived in La Abundancia, the child passed away. The father said: "As I held my son, I was thinking how grateful I was that we had just been sealed in the temple. I know that he is with our Heavenly Father and that we will be with him again someday. Now we are trying to keep all the commandments of our Heavenly Father, because we are thinking of our baby" (*Ensign*, March 1994, 42).

As I thought of their faith, I felt a special warmth for the dedicated missionaries who first contacted those young men from Mistolar, taught them, baptized them, followed up with their families and friends, and helped them catch the vision of eternal families.

Those missionaries, and other leaders, followed the Spirit and did what they needed to do to help those families from Mistolar achieve that lofty goal. For a moment I wished those first missionaries could have been with us in the temple to witness some of the results of their efforts. Then I realized that in fact they were there, shining through those beautiful, faith-filled faces. Wherever they are, all who follow the Spirit and help others in eternally significant ways will enjoy the sweet fruits of their honest, pure efforts.

I thought of the huge amount of planning, patience, and work involved in creating both the treasures of the Tsars and the treasures of the newly sealed families. I admire the skill of the craftsmen in the days of the Tsars, as they took raw material and skillfully fabricated fabulously beautiful robes and jewelry. But I admire infinitely more the craftsmanship, patience, faith, and love of missionaries, home teachers, and leaders all over the world as they skillfully use God's spirit and inspiration to help mold humble souls into glowing families like those we witnessed in the temple.

The Lord will help us wherever we are to provide for our families in the best way possible, both physically and spiritually. He will especially help us to see more clearly how we can use our efforts to build eternal families, rather than merely fabricating diamond-encrusted golden eggs or pearl-edged royal robes. The treasures of the Tsars are well on their way to the rust heap, while the treasures of the families from Mistolar are well on their way to eternal brilliance!

Chapter 20

The One

One assignment during our years in South America took me to a village high in the Andes of northern Chile. While I was there, the stake president requested my assistance in counseling with a bishop who had asked to be released. He told me the bishop had served faithfully and well for two years but felt he could not continue serving because his sixteen-year-old daughter had committed a moral transgression. The daughter had confessed freely and was very repentant, but her father—the bishop—was still angry and embarrassed. He felt sure he could no longer serve effectively as bishop when the whole ward knew of his daughter's mistake.

I suggested we visit this family in their home. The drive to their small ranch was long and dusty. When we finally arrived and entered the home we found it neat, clean, comfortable, and filled with several smiling children. They were overjoyed that we would visit them.

The mother said her husband was away feeding some animals but would return soon. While waiting for him to get back, I visited with the daughter. She was a beautiful girl but seemed very withdrawn. What deep, sad eyes she had! She felt terrible about her misstep, but even worse about the scathing, unforgiving attitude of her father. She loved the Savior and had confidence in His atonement and the opportunity for forgiveness. She had a deep desire to do whatever was necessary to repent fully and be forgiven. She said she felt the love of her Heavenly Father, but not of her earthly father. She pleaded, "What can I do?"

Just then the father returned, and we all gathered for a lovely meal. The father, like many in that area, was of Inca descent. I sensed in him the pride and even appearance of an ancient Inca chief. During the meal he proudly explained the Inca calendar and many other marvelous things from their culture. I was amazed at how conversant he was with the promises to the descendants of Lehi in the Book of Mormon and how strongly he felt about them. As he talked he made no reference to his daughter's situation. I prayed fervently in my heart to know how to help this beautiful family. Finally, an impression came.

After the meal I asked the bishop if just the two of us could go outside to see his animals and talk alone. As we walked together among his prized goats and llamas, I told him that the stake president had explained to me about his daughter and his desire to resign. He became rigid and tense and obviously did not want to talk about it. Feeling more and more confident in the direction I should pursue, I persisted.

I asked if he believed that the Book of Mormon was written to the descendants of Lehi and thus, by extension, to him. He nodded. I then reviewed the account of Alma and his son Corianton and other examples of forgiveness from the Book of Mormon. He listened respectfully, but when I finished he simply said, "I can no longer serve effectively as bishop." Then, with a tone of anger in his voice, he said, "If my own daughter would do this, how can I preach to the members? They will not listen to me. I'm sure they are laughing and saying, 'Control your own daughter before you tell us what to do.'"

I looked him straight in the eye and with full confidence borne of the Spirit said: "If you cannot forgive your own daughter—if you cannot love her in her hour of need and help her through the repentance process—then you cannot have the Spirit of the Lord. If you do not have the Spirit of the Lord, you cannot be a good bishop.

"On the other hand, if you can forgive your very repentant daughter and love and help her through the repentance process, you will have a rich outpouring of the Spirit of the Lord. You will be a better, even more effective bishop. That is what Jesus did. You are His undershepherd and are expected to follow His example. True, a few of the members may be judging you, but mostly they are carefully watching you to see how you react.

"When they see your love for your daughter and feel your testimony of the principles of true repentance and forgiveness—made possible through the atonement of the Savior—I promise you that, rather than turn from you or laugh at you, the members will love, respect, and follow you more than ever. Love begets love; forgiveness begets forgiveness; hope begets hope. As they see these qualities in you, many will come to you with problems of their own that they would not have dared bring up if they had not witnessed your loving, forgiving attitude toward your daughter. Your ability to minister to your flock will thus be strengthened, not weakened.

"The Good Shepherd left the ninety and nine and searched to bring the lost one home. You can be sure the ninety and nine were well aware of where their Shepherd was and what He was doing. Think of the confidence His searching for the lost one gave them! They knew that if they ever strayed, He would search for them also. Your congregation is made up of more than ninety-nine souls, and they are all watching you! Now, what will you do?"

He seemed stunned. For a long time he looked at me—then his lips began to quiver, tears filled his eyes, and I could literally see the "scales of darkness" fall from them (see 2 Nephi 30:6). He asked if we could pray together. During the prayer, the Lord confirmed to him the course he should take. It was difficult and humbling for him to make that "mighty change," but he knew this was the Lord's will. His whole attitude and countenance changed from one of pride, hurt, and anger to one of humility, gratitude, and love.

We returned to the house. He called his daughter, hugged her, and asked her to forgive him for his previous harsh words and unforgiving heart. The mother was overcome. I could tell how much she loved her daughter, yet how much she desired to support her husband. Now, with his change of heart, there was no longer a conflict. Her prayers for both her daughter and her husband had been heard and answered.

As we prepared to leave this humble home, we knelt in prayer with the family. During that prayer the sweet Spirit of the Lord filled every heart. A sacred sense of understanding from the Book of Mormon came to me. I knew that across the ages, ancient prophets had spoken to and been heard by some of their descendants.

As I flew back to Argentina, I wondered if my children and grandchildren felt my love for them and would always feel comfortable about discussing anything with me. I wondered if to some extent I had been a little like the bishop before the eyes of his understanding were opened (see Doctrine and Covenants 76:12). I hoped not.

I realized I needed to keep the spirit of love, forgiveness, kindness, and helpfulness forever uppermost in my life. When problems arise, if any of us are unwilling to talk to our leaders or to listen lovingly to those in trouble, we need to think more of the Savior and strengthen our faith in Him and His atonement. He suffered that we might forgive and be forgiven. What a joy and a responsibility it is to follow Him!

I had seen a proud descendant of Lehi humble himself under the mighty hand of God and bring joy not only to his present family but to generations past and to generations yet to come. I came to understand that forgiving and seeking forgiveness with all our hearts brings a joy that goes far beyond this mortal life.

Chapter 21

THE SHOE-SHINE MAN

I was assigned to organize a new stake from a mission district in La Serena, Chile. Some of the stakes in Chile at that time were struggling to function properly. I was concerned about this and wanted to make sure I did not organize a stake before it was ready.

On the plane from Santiago to La Serena, I reviewed over and over again the statistical information I had received on the La Serena District. I wondered if the district might need a little more time to mature under the guidance of the mission president. I prayed a great deal but did not feel strongly one way or the other. Then just as we landed, a calm feeling came over me. Even though I hadn't received a complete answer, I knew that someway the Lord would make clear to me the direction I should go.

I took a taxi to the downtown hotel where I had arranged to meet the district president. The plane had arrived early, so I still had about an hour before our appointment. It was a pleasant afternoon, and the nearby central plaza looked inviting, so I went for a walk. The plaza was absolutely beautiful with manicured hedges, magnificent trees, and beautiful flowers. I was impressed with all I saw and felt from the polite and helpful people I met.

As I walked on, I began to feel more and more positive about creating the stake, but I still had a few lingering doubts. For some reason my gaze was drawn to an area where a few men were shining shoes. I noticed one man in particular whose body was horribly misshapen. His back and head were bent and twisted in such a way that he could not really look up—only down and to the sides. He appeared to be quite old, but it was hard to tell his age.

I looked at my shoes and, though they didn't really need it, I felt a desire to have this man shine them. I suppose I was partially drawn to him out of a sense of pity or sorrow, but there seemed to be something beyond that pulling me in his direction. I asked him how much for a shine and he told me. It was not much. He smiled as I said that was fine and sat down. He was very efficient and knew exactly what to do. As he worked, we had a wonderful conversation from which I learned much about his family and about La Serena. His skillful hands worked fast, and soon my shoes really shone! He asked if I felt my shoes looked all right. I told him they looked even better than the day I bought them. He smiled and held out his hand.

I gave him an amount that was many times what we had agreed on and told him that since he had done such a good job and I had learned so much, I would like him to keep the difference. He quickly shook his head, dug into his money sack, and got the exact change. I again asked him to keep the difference. He turned his head at the best angle he could, stretched out his hand with the change, and said, "Take it. I want you to know that I am a shoe shiner, not a beggar!"

I realized that the best way to help this man at that moment was to take the change and thank him for his integrity. As I did, I gave him a verbal blessing and invited him and his family to our meeting on Sunday. He appreciated both. Someone else walked up just then, and he was quickly back to work.

As I returned slowly to the hotel, I knew I had my answer: A stake would be created in La Serena. How appropriate, I thought, to feel so serene in La Serena.

On Sunday we created the stake. I looked and looked for the shoe-shine man and his family. Even though I did not see their physical presence, I felt their influence. As I spoke to the congregation, I told of the integrity I had felt from one of the inhabitants of La Serena and challenged them to follow that example of integrity in their callings, in their tithe paying, and in their families. I felt certain they would.

God's messengers can and do come in many different forms, anytime, anywhere. American poet and journalist Nathaniel Parker Willis (1806–1867) expressed it well: "Nature's noblemen are everywhere, in town and out of town, gloved and rough handed, rich and poor. Prejudice against a lord because he is a lord, is losing the chance of finding a good fellow, as much as prejudice against a ploughman because he is a ploughman."

Our duty is to not prejudge anyone or any situation, but to listen to and obey the promptings of the Spirit. Nearly two decades after the creation of the La Serena Stake, it continues to function well and I continue to feel serene about that decision.

Chapter 22

HONORABLY RELEASED

During a stake conference in Santiago, Chile, the mission president told us of a returned sister missionary who was very ill in the hospital. We felt prompted to visit her, so we rearranged some meetings and went to the hospital. I have learned that when we obey such promptings, we find ourselves in places and situations where the Lord can use us to help someone and where we can receive the insights and blessings we need.

As we entered the missionary's room, we were impressed with her beautiful attitude. Her body was very weak, but her spirit was unusually strong. She told us a little of her history and requested a blessing. In the process of blessing her, we received the greater blessing. There was such a special spirit of reverence, beauty, and assurance about her that we seemed to be in another world. Our visit was relatively short, but strangely we felt we had known her forever.

We left the hospital very subdued, realizing we had been in the presence of true greatness. The Spirit of God (the pure spirit of love) was so intense as to leave us almost weak with wonder. I asked myself, *Why can't we be more like her—full of love and gratitude?*

About two weeks later, the same mission president called us in Argentina and informed us that this sister had just passed away. He said some of her last words were expressions of gratitude for our visit. The call came just as I was leaving for a stake conference in a distant part of Buenos Aires. As we traveled to the conference, I felt this young sister's presence and goodness such that although I had not been physically present when she passed away, I felt as though I had been. Under the influence of the Spirit, I was shown with certainty and clarity what took place as this sister made the transition to the other side of the veil.

So strong were these feelings that I felt impressed to tell her story at the conference. I explained to the congregation that I would speak of her life from what I had learned from the mission president and our visit with her, but I would speak of her passing as given me by the Spirit. This was my message:

Sister Meha had always wanted to serve a mission. She was an active, vivacious, healthy young woman. When she turned twenty-one, she was thrilled to receive a call to serve a mission in Chile. On her mission she bore her testimony often, taught the truth with sweetness and firmness, served well, and had the power of heaven with her. Through her efforts many souls followed the path of faith, repentance, and baptism, which opened great doors of opportunity for them. As her mission progressed, her testimony of the Savior and His atoning sacrifice for everyone became stronger and stronger. She often quoted 2 Nephi 9:20–24:

"O how great the holiness of our God! For he knoweth all things, and there is not anything save he knows it.

"And he cometh into the world that he may save all men if they will hearken unto his voice; for behold, he suffereth the pains of all men, yea, the pains of every living creature, both men, women, and children, who belong to the family of Adam.

"And he suffereth this that the resurrection might pass upon all men, that all might stand before him at the great and judgment day.

"And he commandeth all men that they must repent, and be baptized in his name, having perfect faith in the Holy One of Israel, or they cannot be saved in the kingdom of God.

"And if they will not repent and believe in his name, and be baptized in his name, and endure to the end, they must be damned; for the Lord God, the Holy One of Israel, has spoken it."

She knew her Savior. She expressed her love for Him with such conviction that her contacts could actually feel it. Her radiant testimony and pure love made a deep impression on all around her.

Toward the end of her mission, this sister began to feel very tired. Some days she had difficulty getting up and going about her work. She talked to her mission president, who suggested she see a doctor. The doctor said that since the fatigue was only occasional, it might be best for her to wait and see her doctor at home. Under these circumstances, her mission president suggested that she be released now, which was a month early. She chose to stay and finish her mission.

She worked extra hard that last month, and two more families joined the Church. When she returned home, she felt better. Her stake president welcomed her home. He gave her the mission president's letter commending her for her work and extending to her an honorable release. How she treasured that letter!

She began attending college, but the spells of fatigue returned. Her doctor ordered several tests and within a few days told her that she had a rare form of cancer. She was sent to an excellent hospital and was treated with everything medically possible.

She became so extremely thin that the phrase "skin and bones" had literal meaning. Despite this, her spirit remained buoyant. Her smile was so radiant that she literally glowed with goodness, kindness, and gratitude. In a priesthood blessing she was told that her Heavenly Father knew her, knew her situation, and was pleased with her mission and her attitude. He would see to it that what was best for everyone would be done.

Soon the doctors said there was nothing more they could do, so the family decided to bring her home. How she enjoyed those last days with her family, and how blessed her family, friends, and neighbors were by being around her! Her body grew steadily weaker while her spirit grew steadily stronger. Over and over she expressed appreciation for her mission, for her mission president, for her parents, and for all those who had helped her. There was no complaining.

Early one morning she called her family to her bedside. She again expressed her love and appreciation for everyone and for all their help. She asked them to tell me and Jean how much she appreciated our visit and to tell the mission president and his wife how much she appreciated all they had done for her. She expressed her love for the Savior and then asked, "Could you please bring me my letter of release?" They brought it to her.

Even though she had read this letter a hundred times, she asked them to read it once more. She beamed as they did. When they read the words, "You are hereby honorably released," the light of her countenance sent forth rays of love that they literally felt. Everyone was in tears. Her smile was so deep, so intense, so pure, so glorious they sensed she was seeing things more beautiful than she could describe. She took the letter, clutched it to her heart, and softly repeated the words, "You are hereby honorably released." Then she closed her eyes and was gone.

The light and love so palpably present around this sister reached out and touched everyone, including those in this

Group of Chilean missionaries.

conference in Argentina. Her love and goodness gave us all great understanding. The most important thing in this life is to love and obey God with all our heart, might, mind, and strength, and to love our neighbors as ourselves. We show that love by helping others, as Jesus did and does. How beautifully this sister loved. Her teaching, testifying, and loving brought many—including herself—to Him.

For some, the period of earthly probation is shorter than for others, but the opportunities given us to prove ourselves by developing and practicing Christlike love are sufficient for everyone. Isn't it fascinating how anyone, anytime, anywhere, even under difficult circumstances, can do something to bless those around them? How grateful I am to have known and felt the heavenly influence of this wonderful Chilean sister!

Chapter 23

A Christmas Remembered

I think most parents at some point look at their children and realize how quickly they are growing and how soon they will be gone. They wonder: Have I prepared them for life? Do they know how much I love them? I was having those feelings one Christmas years ago. As I looked at our daughters, I saw their mother's goodness sparkle from their eyes. What a blessing they would be to their own families as they followed their mother's footsteps.

It is a huge responsibility to be a mother in Zion! I wanted to help my girls feel the significance of their future motherhood and the importance of bringing the joy to their families that Jean had brought to ours. I thought of all the things I could say to help them understand these truths, but in the end I realized that what we *do* is the best sermon and has the longest lasting and the most powerful influence. I had such deep feelings of love and gratitude for Jean and the children that I thought maybe the best thing to do was to express these feelings in writing so I could share them with the children when they were a little older. I didn't know it at the time, but this turned out to be one of our last Christmases in Idaho for many years. Here is what I later wrote:

Christmas in Idaho is beautiful—snowy and cold outside, snug and warm inside. It was Christmas Eve, and our family of young children was putting on our traditional Christmas pageant from Luke, chapter two. One of the children read from the Bible while the others played the roles of Mary, Joseph, the innkeeper, shepherds, wise men, or the star. Dad, by tradition, was the donkey so Mary could ride him and Joseph could lead him. How the children enjoyed that! The youngest child was always the baby Jesus. Reverence and goodness glistened from every eye as carols were sung and the beautiful story of the Savior's birth was reenacted and felt anew. The mother and the Baby were the center of it all. After the pageant, each child opened one present, hung up a stocking, then scampered off to bed, hopefully to sleep till morning. During the night Santa worked his magic.

Early Christmas morning we gathered for family prayer and our traditional Christmas breakfast of grapefruit, milk, and sweet rolls. Afterwards, everyone lined up from youngest to oldest to go into the family room to see what Santa had brought.

How do you capture the wide eyes of surprise and the gleeful squeals of joy when a child sees a long-hoped-for pair of ice skates

The Groberg family in hand-sewn PJs and robes, Christmas, early 1970s.

or a new sweater or an anticipated game? I suppose it can be recorded only in the heart.

The greatest excitement was when the presents the children had made by themselves were opened. "Open this one first, Mom," giggled a four-year-old.

"Okay! Oh, what lovely dolls! [empty spools of thread—colored and dressed] I can see a nose and a mouth, and, guess what? I can see eyes like yours, only yours are brighter!" (As were everyone's.)

What joy comes from giving and receiving with sincere thought and appreciation! Size and price make no difference. Everyone felt loved as each responded to the true spirit of Christmas. Part of heaven had come to earth. I was trying to absorb all the laughter and love I could, for the next day I was to leave on a long trip.

I was serving as a Regional Representative and had been assigned to hold several stake conferences in the South Pacific. To meet the schedule of meetings, I needed to leave the day after Christmas and be gone for nearly three weeks. I wanted to do my duty in the South Pacific, but knew how much I would miss being with my family! Christmas Day was marvelous and memorable. I left early the next morning, flying first to Samoa for two conferences, then to Fiji for two more, then to Tonga for the last two (in those days we often held conferences midweek). All of the conferences were wonderful, but as the last day dawned, I found myself thinking more and more about my wife and children. I wondered how each was doing. I knew God was in charge and I shouldn't worry about them, but that is easier said than done. I hoped I wasn't feeling sorry for myself.

Actually, I loved being with the Polynesian people. I loved their singing. I loved to feel the strength of their testimonies and the power of their faith in song and sermon and prayer. What spiritual giants they were! Even the crumbs from their towering table of faith were a feast to me. As I reflected upon my love for the Polynesians, for the Savior, and for my family in Idaho, the thought came to me that although Polynesia and Idaho may be contradictory in terms of location, weather, and culture, they are complementary in terms of faith, goodness, and love.

As the last meeting ended, I expressed my love and testimony, embraced those wonderful Saints, and caught the plane home. I was very tired but very happy.

During the flight home of seventeen-plus hours I reflected on the marvelous spiritual feast I had partaken of for the last three weeks. I wondered how I could most effectively share it with my wife and children. Then I thought of all they had been doing during those same three weeks. My love for the Polynesians was deep, but my love for Jean and our family was even deeper.

It was late on the snowy night of January 15 when I landed in Idaho Falls. Only hours before, I had been enjoying a temperature of 85 degrees; now it was 10 below zero. That made no difference, however, for the warmth of love was the same. Jean met me at the airport. She was expecting another child, and as I embraced her I felt secure and loved and very blessed.

When we arrived home, I looked around and saw a clean, orderly house, sleeping children safely tucked in bed, and a beautiful wife standing by my side. I looked at Jean. I thought of all the meals she had cooked, the clothes she had washed, the diapers she had changed, the misunderstandings she had settled, the stories she had read, the prayers she had said, and everything else she had done without complaining in order to keep the family going while I was away. I felt her love and goodness and asked myself: *How can you put a value on a good wife and mother?* The answer came immediately: *You can't. You just stand back and marvel at the blessing God gave you when He gave you Jean.*

I thought of the words of one of the wisest of men trying to describe such a woman: "Her price is far above rubies. The heart of her husband doth safely trust in her. . . . [She] worketh willingly with her hands. . . . She riseth also while it is yet night, and giveth meat to her household. . . . She stretcheth out her hand to the poor; yea, she reacheth forth her hands to the needy. She is not afraid of the snow. . . . Strength and honour are her clothing. . . . She openeth her mouth with wisdom; and in her tongue is the law of kindness. She looketh well to the ways of her household, and eateth not the bread of idleness. Her children arise up, and call her blessed; her husband also, and he praiseth her" (Proverbs 31:10–28).

I said to myself, *I wish Solomon could have known Jean. He could have written so much more.*

I looked at Jean again and thought of her mother and her mother's mother. I thought of my mother and her mother. I thought of mothers everywhere: the believing mother of Joseph Smith, the humble mother of Jesus, the courageous mother of Moses, and on back through time to faithful mother Eve. What examples of love and faith! What a powerful magnet a mother's love is and always will be, to draw the best from everyone! What great blessings flow through faithful women—at Christmastime or anytime—at home or anywhere. How much more we should all do to praise and help our mothers and our wives, the mothers of our children.

I tried to explain these feelings to Jean, but found myself simply holding her tightly and quietly whispering: "It's good to be with you. It's good to be home!"

People and places we visited when we were serving anytime, anywhere.

LOMI STREET
DESING

Chapter 24

The Honolulu Airport

When we moved to Hawaii, I immediately began working on my assignment to organize the new Hawaii—Pacific Islands Area of the Church, which included all of the stakes and missions in Hawaii, Tahiti, Tonga, Samoa, Fiji, Guam, and many other Pacific islands. This vast area known as Micronesia, Melanesia, and Polynesia is mostly water, but includes thousands of beautiful islands inhabited by warm and wonderful people—many of whom are faithful members of the Church. I was overwhelmed with the distances and the scope of the assignment, but I learned that the Lord always gives us the help and direction we need to solve challenges and properly fulfill our assignments. Here are two examples.

First: For the previous seven years I had served as a Regional Representative, with assignments mostly in the South Pacific. Jean always drove me to and from the airport in Idaho Falls. When we arrived in Hawaii, she continued that practice. Two of our daughters attended Kalani High School and could watch the younger children for the hour or so it took Jean to drive me to and from the Honolulu airport. We quickly found, however, that things were very different in Hawaii from the way they were in Idaho

Falls. Nearly all of my flights to Samoa, Tonga, and the other islands left and returned during the wee hours of the morning. I didn't feel right about Jean being out alone in that big city during those hours.

This uncomfortable feeling persisted, so I asked the Lord what I should do. An unmistakable impression came to me that Jean should stay home with the children and I should ask the missionaries to take me to and from the airport during those midnight hours. I worked with the mission president, who happily agreed to help. Soon we had a rotating schedule of missionaries who lived in close proximity to our home and the airport and were willing and anxious to perform this unusual assignment. For the remainder of our time in Hawaii, two missionaries—often sleepy but always there—faithfully transported me to and from the airport.

This would probably be handled differently today, but it worked well then. I had some wonderful conversations with the elders as they faithfully rendered that service. Through the years I have met some of those missionaries or members of their families at stake conferences and other settings. They always express the joy they felt and continue to feel from carrying out that particular assignment. Isn't it amazing to recognize the varied opportunities the Lord opens for us to give and receive help?

Most assignments come in regular ways and at normal times, but sometimes they come in unusual ways and at inconvenient times. I have come to know that it doesn't matter how, when, or where we are asked to serve, only that we serve with all our hearts.

Second: As difficult as it was for me to leave Jean and the children, sometimes for long periods of time, it was even more difficult for them to be left alone. I say left alone, yet I know that when any of us are doing our duty, we and our loved ones are never really alone. The Lord is always there to help. Jean has always done her duty with faith, love, and kindness, and the Lord

Jennie holding Emily.

has blessed her. I know that rearing a large family in a new location, with her husband gone to faraway places much of the time, was a daunting task for Jean, but she always found comfort in the Lord's promise to help us in our righteous needs.

When someone needs help, I wonder if the Lord doesn't look around to see who is humble enough, capable enough, close enough, and willing enough to hear the promptings of His Spirit and follow them. When He finds such a person, He uses him or her to accomplish that particular help. Often a child is the most available, the most humble, and the most reachable.

Jean writes of a time in Hawaii when extra help was needed and received:

It was one of those mornings when nothing went right. We had overslept, the older girls had missed their ride to early morning seminary, shoes were lost, books were missing. There were long lists of complaints, short tempers, and spilt milk. Dad was away on a trip and I had long since "lost my cool." When the tumult tapered off as the seventh school child was hustled out the door with the hassled reminder, "Hurry! You're late!" I crunched across the cereal-covered floor to get the broom and start the "reconstruction process" on our local disaster area.

Our bright-eyed three-year-old, Jennie Marie, sensed my frustration and wanted to help. She brought in her favorite storybook and with deep compassion said, "I'll read you a story, Mommy."

The book was called A Present for the Princess. *It starts out, "Once upon a time there was a little princess. She was beautiful and blue-eyed and bonnie and everybody loved her." The next page shows a king and queen proudly looking on while a teenage princess is walking with care as she balances a book on her head. The caption says, "Her father was a king, her mother was a queen, and she had a big sister who was practicing to be a queen."*

That is how the book tells it. But on that morning Jennie Marie's version went like this: "Once upon a time, there was a beautiful little princess . . ." Then when she came to the page showing the king and queen and the big sister, Jennie said, "The king was practicing to be a father and the queen was practicing to be a mother."

Seldom has any message hit me with more force. Well, "Mother Jean," you surely do have a lot of practicing to do! Becoming worthy parents does take a lot of practicing. No matter how tired we are—how rebellious or difficult they are—we have covenanted to keep trying, keep praying, keep loving, keep smiling, keep encouraging—and never give up.

The Lord does bless our consistent efforts and desires to do what is right, despite all the times we fall short. He wants us to be righteous children, worthy husbands or wives, and successful parents, and since we cannot do it on our own, the Lord promises that "He shall feed his flock . . . and shall gently lead those that are with young" (Isaiah 40:11).

* * *

Jean made it through that storm and many others. We have learned together how important it is to keep trying and keep practicing to become better mothers and fathers, sons and daughters, and follow the promptings of the Lord's Spirit anytime, anywhere, in any situation. We know that as we place our full trust in the Lord, He will "gently lead" us into His eternal fold.

Chapter 25

OLD FRIEND

In 1978 we were called to leave Hawaii and move to Utah where, among other things, I was given the assignment to chair the Church-sponsored World Conference on Records to be held in August of 1980. The purpose of the conference was to gather archivists and genealogists from all over the world to share information and establish friendly relations. The basic groundwork had been laid, but myriads of details had to be pulled together to make it a success. Over the next two years, the amount of planning, coordinating, budgeting, visa arranging, and every other conceivable element of this historic event was mind-boggling. Hundreds of dedicated people put forth tremendous effort along with great faith and constant prayers. Despite the daunting nature of the task, I knew that with the assignment and support of the Church leaders, God would guide us and His purposes would be fulfilled, which they were.

To give an idea of the magnitude of this conference: There were several hundred presenters from nearly fifty countries, and more than 11,000 people attended the various sessions held over four days. Seldom have I felt a better spirit of cooperation and certainty of purpose. Every person and every entity involved in any

Part of over 11,000 attendees at World Conference on Records in Salt Lake City, 1980, where Alex Haley, well-known author of Roots, *was one of the speakers.*

way with the conference worked harmoniously together despite the many challenges inherent in such a large-scale, international undertaking. The hand of the Lord was plainly evident in all that was accomplished. Everything about the conference was a marvelous success.

It is not possible to measure all the good that resulted from the World Conference on Records, but one experience involving the delegates from the People's Republic of China had particular significance to me. In 1980 the Cold War was in full freeze and the iron and bamboo curtains were much more than figures of speech. Great care was taken to protect the delicate situation between the delegates from mainland China and those from Taiwan. Fortunately, with the Lord's blessing, no major problems arose.

Jean and I enjoyed meeting the representatives from other countries at the conference, but for some reason we developed a special bond with the delegation from the People's Republic of China. Their group consisted of three archivists and one "government representative/translator." We invited the four of them to come to our home, meet our family, and have dinner with us.

They were a little hesitant, but when we assured them no one but our family and the four of them would attend, they agreed. We had a wonderful evening. As we finished, the senior archivist said through his interpreter: "We have eaten in your home and have met your family. You are now our friend. If you ever come to China, please let us know. We would like to renew our friendship, eat a meal with you, and help you any way we can. Thank you for this conference, thank you for this meal, and thank you for being our friend." We felt a warm and sincere spirit from this man and his colleagues. Despite the misunderstandings and suspicions toward Communist China that were common at that time, we felt only love and respect for these wonderful gentlemen.

Now, fast-forward about fifteen years, to when Jean and I and our youngest daughter were living in Hong Kong where I was serving in the Asia Area Presidency. In our assignment we had visited China many times and continued to have warm feelings toward those good people. The Church was not allowed to proselyte, but the many expatriate members living in China could meet together, so we had several strong branches there.

Earlier an agreement had been worked out with the Chinese government on sharing genealogical records. It included authorization to set up a Church-sponsored reading room in the genealogical sections of the major libraries in Beijing and Shanghai. However, for some unknown reason we were kept from implementing the agreement. We tried every way we knew to understand why they would not allow us to proceed. We suspected that they might have some lingering suspicions as to what our intentions were in establishing these rooms, but we were not sure. The reading rooms in their libraries were vitally important as the first step in implementing the exchange agreement. I knew that moving forward with this program would be important in helping the spirit of Elijah more fully enter this great country. I suppose Satan understood that also and was trying to block or delay it.

Months went by with no progress. It was very frustrating. Then, one day in Hong Kong, Jean reminded me about our Chinese archivist friends. As she spoke, I felt again that warm feeling we had experienced fifteen years earlier. My prayers confirmed that we should pursue this. I excitedly called the area family history representative and asked if he remembered the World Conference on Records held in Salt Lake City fifteen years earlier and particularly the delegation from mainland China. He remembered the conference, and said he would check with the Family History Department in Salt Lake to get more information on the Chinese delegates. Old records are often hard to access, even for record keepers, but eventually the names of these three men were found. I asked him if he could check to see if our friends were still alive, and if so, could he contact them and let them know that we would be visiting China soon and would like to renew our friendship?

After much searching, he discovered that one of the three had died, but the other two were still alive. We made contact with them and received word back that the next time we came to Beijing they would like to meet us and treat us to a full-course "Beijing Duck" dinner. We learned that in China when government officials, such as these archivists, retire, they turn things over to their replacements but often stay on as advisors—thus continuing their influence and sharing their experience. With this information in mind, we arranged a mutually acceptable date for our trip to Beijing. We also let our friends know of the difficulties we were encountering with the Beijing and Shanghai libraries.

On the appointed day, we were treated to an elaborate dinner in downtown Beijing. What an evening! We found that our friends had invited to dinner the officials currently in charge of the libraries. One of our friends acted as the senior spokesman. Now bowed with age but still clear in mind, he told of the wonderful World Conference on Records in Salt Lake City. He spoke

In front of a National Library of China.

fondly of meeting our family and eating in our home. Throughout his remarks, the key phrase seemed to be "old friend." Over and over, he emphasized it. I felt to say, "Yes, old friends and good friends."

Within a few days of this meal, we received word that we could fully implement our genealogy agreement. Suddenly, instead of putting us off, the local Chinese leaders were wondering how soon we could start and what they could do to help. In short order, the reading rooms were functioning both in Beijing and in Shanghai. A mutually agreed-upon plaque was placed at the entrance to each room recognizing the Church by name as a contributor to the project.

I am certain that this is not the end of the story. The Lord knows the beginning from the end. He also knows all the paths and pieces along the way. He knows what needs to happen now so that something else can happen later. He puts plans in motion that, when followed, create marvelous results. We cannot see or understand fully what He sees and understands. Our part is to always be kind and thoughtful in any situation, under any condition, and realize that anyone, anywhere can be an instrument in His hands to bring about His purposes.

Chapter 26

FAITH FULFILLED

All honest, pure faith is fulfilled eventually. Sometimes it takes longer than other times, but God is always aware and fulfills our faith at the time best for us. Think of Job, or Simeon and Anna (see Luke 2:25–38). Sometimes the fulfillment is beyond the veil, as in the case of Lazarus and the rich man (see Luke 16:19–25). If our faith, our love, and our prayers are humble, honest, and pure, they are never lost or wasted, and they always bring eternal blessings. We must never become impatient or expect anything that is in any way contrary to God's will. If our faith is pure, we will never give up but will endure in faith to the end. Here are two examples of long-held faith being fulfilled.

First: While we were living in Hong Kong, the time arrived for the dedication of the Hong Kong Temple. What excitement filled the members' hearts as it was announced that Presidents Gordon B. Hinckley and Thomas S. Monson and a few others would come for the dedication! Among the most excited yet humble members were many of the Filipina sisters who lived and worked in Hong Kong. The majority of these women worked hard as domestics and sent most of their money home to their families in the Philippines.

One sister, who was representative of many, had a great desire to feel the strength of President Hinckley's calling and testimony. We will call this woman Eva. A recent convert to the Church, Eva asked over and over again what she could do to help prepare for the dedication. We organized a choir of Filipino members to sing at one of the sessions. In this way they would be close to the prophet and feel the strength of his love and testimony. They practiced and practiced, but Eva wanted to do even more. She arranged her work schedule so she could come to assist in the final cleaning of the temple. She also volunteered to help in serving the special guests and washing the dishes.

The big day came. In the session where the Filipino choir sang, it was as though heavenly choirs had come to Hong Kong. When President Hinckley spoke, he turned to the choir and, with tears in his eyes, blessed them for their faithfulness, their love, and their sacrifice for their families. It was truly a time of fulfillment as through their tears they felt the warmth of his love, the strength of his testimony, and the power of his prophetic calling.

Eva and all of the choir members felt that their faith and their long hours of practicing were fulfilled. Eva could imagine no more, but still went the extra mile in serving and clearing the light refreshments provided for the Brethren and their wives between sessions. She hoped only to be of service and perhaps to get a closer glimpse of the prophet.

Then it happened! Just as she was going about happily serving, she came face to face with President Hinckley. He stopped, looked directly at Eva, thanked her for her service—and then he reached out and spontaneously gave her a fatherly hug and words of encouragement. She could hardly believe what had happened, but she knew how much God loved her and was aware of her sacrifice and her faith.

Sincere, humble faith is always rewarded in God's own time and way. We must never give up and never seek more than the privilege of helping—no matter where or how or to whom.

Second: Near the end of President Ezra Taft Benson's earthly life, there were times when he was not able to do very much, at least as far as mortals could observe. He had a great love for the Book of Mormon and heeded the Lord's promptings to encourage its greater use. Among those deeply affected by the teachings of this great prophet, particularly as they related to the Book of Mormon, were a group of Tongan Saints living in California.

One day at Church headquarters, I received a phone call from this group of Tongan priesthood and Relief Society leaders. They had come with no advance notice bringing a handmade quilt for President Benson. They wondered if I could arrange for them to give it to him, or if I could get it to him some other way. They had heard he was not feeling well, and in their humble way they wanted to make sure he was warm enough. The custom of giving tapa cloth or quilts to keep one warm dates back into ancient Tongan history and is a sign of respect, concern, and love.

I explained that President Benson was not in his office, but was resting at his home. I told them he was very weak and could have no visitors. They understood and asked, if they brought the quilt to me, could I get it to President Benson? They emphasized again how concerned they were about his illness and how they wanted to make sure he was warm enough. They also wanted him to know of their love and faith and prayers for him. I assured them that he was receiving excellent care, which included making sure he was warm enough. I was about to say that I doubted another quilt would help, when my voice suddenly stopped and I found myself saying, "Please come to the church parking lot and I will arrange to have your quilt delivered to President Benson's secretary, who will deliver it to President Benson and tell him of your love and your desire that he be warm enough." As those words came out of my mouth in Tongan, I realized that it was the warmth of their love, more than the warmth of their quilt, that they wanted him to feel.

I hurriedly called President Benson's personal secretary, who just happened to be in his office. He said the president was unable to receive visitors, but we could have this group come to his office and leave the quilt there. I met the group of about a dozen faithful Tongan members in the parking area of the Administration Building, and we went to President Benson's office on the first floor.

His secretary graciously showed them the First Presidency Board Room, then said they could go into President Benson's vacant office and see the prophet's desk and chair. This faithful group of awestruck members entered his office with such deep reverence you could hardly hear a breath. There were muffled sobs of joy as they whispered in their native tongue, "We are standing where the prophet has stood. We are seeing the chair where he sits, and the desk he has worked from." They used phrases indicating that they could hardly believe this experience was real. They whispered how strongly they felt the presence of the Spirit of the Lord, and how deeply they felt President Benson's love.

With profound reverence and glistening eyes, they carefully refolded the quilt and lovingly placed it upon his desk. In hushed tones they again expressed their gratitude for the privilege of being in the prophet's office. They told me they felt his spirit close to them and knew he felt their love. They were fully satisfied. As they looked once more around the office, I noticed their eyes lingering on their quilt—the physical embodiment of their deep love for the prophet—lying regally on his desk.

As they were filing slowly out of the president's office, the phone rang. President Benson's secretary answered it and in a moment motioned me to have the Tongans wait. When he hung up, he said, "Something unusual has happened." He explained that the call was from President Benson's private nurse, who asked if there were someone there to see the president. The nurse explained that that day the president had not felt like getting out of bed, and he had no appointments. However, for some reason he had just told the nurse he must get up and get dressed, because someone was coming to see him. The secretary confirmed that he had no appointments scheduled. But when the nurse explained how strongly the prophet felt that someone was coming to visit him, the secretary said that there was a group of Tongans who had a quilt for him. If the president felt strong enough, he would have them come to his apartment and present it to him personally.

President Ezra Taft Benson as he looked when he received the quilt from the Tongan Saints.

You can imagine the Tongans' amazement and joy when they heard this miraculous message. They reverently took the quilt to President Benson's apartment. As the door was opened, there sat President Benson, all dressed and ready to greet them. With hushed tones, full hearts, and tear-filled eyes, they explained why they were there. They expressed their love for the prophet, unfolded the beautiful quilt, and presented it to him, saying they hoped it would help keep him warm. He held his hands out wide and said, "For me? For me? You made it for me?"

"Yes," they replied. "For you—to keep you warm."

"For me—for me—you did it for me? Thank you. Thank you. Thank you."

That was about the end of his strength. The group left, humbled, fulfilled, and strengthened in a way impossible to describe. On the way back there was very little talking. No one laughed or commented on the marvelous thing that had just happened. They only looked at one another in wonder and amazement at God's love to them. As I helped this little band return to their vans, I had the feeling that I had seen a glimpse of how the humble shepherds of long ago reacted both on the plains and before the manger as they expressed quiet gratitude and wondrous awe for the miraculous message of God's great love for them.

I doubt this event could have happened in any other way. I believe one of the reasons it happened was that this group had worked hours and hours to prepare something to help the prophet, expecting nothing but the privilege of expressing their love and their hope that the ailing prophet be kept warm. Their faith had already been fulfilled as they began to leave his office. The rest was God's miraculous way of adding even more fulfillment to their humble faith, love, and desire to help.

I am confident that that is God's way. We do all we can—we love, we serve, we help, we try to keep others warm, especially with our love and concern. We feel the joy from such service, and our faith in God is fulfilled. Then, filled with gratitude and seeking only to continue helping, we sometimes experience occasions when God cannot restrain His love, but adds even more fulfillment, "good measure, pressed down, and shaken together, and running over" (Luke 6:38).

Chapter 27

NOW I BELONG

The Hong Kong Temple had been dedicated for about a year when, according to a prearranged schedule, the turnover of Hong Kong from Great Britain back to China took place. The government of China had approved a local leader and agreed that essentially everything would stay the same in Hong Kong for the next fifty years. Some people, both in Salt Lake City and in the world generally, had concerns about how things would work in Hong Kong after the turnover. Those of us in Hong Kong were not worried, as we felt sure the Chinese government would keep its word.

The Hong Kong Temple was operating well and proving to be a great blessing to the people of the Asia area. Groups from Singapore, Malaysia, Thailand, Sri Lanka, India, Mongolia, and other countries came and received the blessings of sacred ordinances. What a joy it was to help them and to share in the warmth and joy they experienced from the temple. The first family from Mongolia to be sealed in the temple is a good example.

This wonderful Mongolian family arrived just as we were finishing an area-wide training meeting in the area offices in Hong Kong. I asked this family if they would sing for the leaders who had gathered from all over Asia, as well as some from Salt Lake City.

Even though we didn't understand the Mongolian words as they sang "I Am a Child of God," we understood their meaning. The glow from these good people's faces and the few translated comments given before and after their song, in which they expressed their love for the gospel, their excitement about being sealed in the temple, and their desire to be a family forever, spoke to the hearts of all present.

We could see the hearts of those priesthood leaders melt as their determination to do and be better glistened from their eyes. They knew that the desired end result of all they did in their Church service was to lead individuals and families to the temple. They understood that the whole purpose of the Church, and even of life, is to bring people to where they are worthy to enter the temple and become eternal families. I felt the power of God and absolutely knew that all would be well with the recently dedicated temple in Hong Kong.

At about this same time, which was shortly before the turnover of Hong Kong back to China, a member of the First Presidency came for a regional conference. We arranged to meet with the newly appointed leader of Hong Kong. He was gracious and thoughtful, and as we asked specific questions about missionary visas, proselyting privileges, meetinghouse usage, and the sanctity of our temple, he simply smiled and stated: "However these things are done today, that is the way they will continue. You have my word." Even though this was a good reassurance, it was a distant second to the spiritual assurance I had received when the Mongolian family sang "I Am a Child of God."

The turnover itself was a study in British "pomp and circumstance" and Chinese pageantry and pragmatism. Every event was magnificent. The bands, the singing, the dragon dancing, the marching, and all the history of the ages of Asia seemed to culminate in this historic event. It rained heavily when the British flag was lowered and the Chinese and Hong Kong flags were raised. I was impressed by Prince Charles as he spoke, representing Britain. He refused an umbrella, stood steady and erect in the pouring rain, and delivered a masterful discourse. There was, of course, some nostalgia as one of the last remnants of the far-flung British Empire returned to its homeland. I was equally touched by the Chinese response, especially the thousands of young Chinese dancers who paid no heed to the rain but carried out their beautifully choreographed movements with skill and enthusiasm.

Some of the outside press tried to make a big deal of the Chinese troops that were sent to Hong Kong. But facts are more powerful than fiction, and every part of the turnover proved to run smoothly and as had been agreed. When we woke up the day after the turnover, everything was just the way it had been the day before, and it continued that way.

The Sunday after the turnover, in a fast and testimony meeting, the feelings and testimonies of many resonated in all of our hearts. One particular testimony, born by a Hong Kong Chinese woman to her sisters in Relief Society where she felt she could safely share her intimate feelings, revealed sentiments not previously appreciated.

This sister had been born and raised in Hong Kong. Her passport was British, and the Union Jack flew over her homeland, but she never felt British. She knew she was Chinese. She went away to school and married an American. They were both active members of the Church, which brought her great comfort, yet there was still an empty space in her heart. When their schooling was finished, they lived in Hong Kong for a while when it was still British. Later they moved to America, but she was not American and didn't feel comfortable there. They lived in England for a time, but she still didn't seem to fit in. Then her husband's work

Hong Kong Temple.

brought them back to Hong Kong not long before the turnover of Hong Kong to China.

Now, with quiet simplicity and deep emotion, she expressed gratitude for the recent return of her homeland to China, saying: "For the first time in my life, I feel like I belong. I am home. I know who I am. I am Chinese and I live in China. But even more important than that, I am a member of The Church of Jesus Christ of Latter-day Saints. I have been sealed in the temple—and now we have a temple in China. Living here in Chinese Hong Kong, I can say: Now I belong—I am whole—I am home." As I contemplated her simple testimony of truth, it seemed I could hear millions say the same thing after joining the Church or receiving temple blessings.

A few days later we attended the temple. As we entered that sacred edifice, I was overwhelmed with a deep feeling of goodness and fulfillment. I stopped for a moment and listened. It was as though I could hear the temple itself breathing the words, "Yes, this is where I belong! I am ready to bless the lives of millions and millions and millions—in China and all of Asia." I know the Lord puts His temples where they belong. I hope we will do more to help everyone, everywhere, including ourselves, come to where we really belong.

Chapter 28

SEEING LIGHTS

During the years we lived in Hong Kong, Jean and I went to India many times to hold Church meetings and visit with government officials on various issues. It was a joy to be with the wonderful people of India and to feel the Lord's influence among them. I will always remember one visit that proved to be unusual, enlightening, and life changing.

On this particular trip I traveled alone while Jean stayed with our youngest daughter, Emily, who was attending high school in Hong Kong. I spent over a week holding meetings with the mission president, the missionaries, and hundreds of members throughout India.

India is a big country, and every day my schedule kept me busy from early morning to late night. It was strenuous but exhilarating. I felt the goodness of the members and the missionaries, who were always smiling and had powerful testimonies and a deep love for the Lord and His work. Despite the heavy schedule, a different bed each night, crowded flights, strange and exotic foods, large crowds, and unusual sights, sounds, and smells, I felt strengthened and buoyed up by the spiritual progress I saw and felt among these humble people.

When we concluded our last meeting, the mission president drove me to the airport in New Delhi, where I caught a plane shortly after midnight for the six-hour flight back to Hong Kong. I felt fine as I boarded the plane, but once we were in the air I was seized by a sudden and violent illness, possibly some type of food poisoning. I began throwing up in a way that seemed to turn my whole insides out. Fortunately, there were very few people where I was seated, so I was able to get back and forth to the lavatory as needed.

I hoped the illness would pass quickly, but instead it got worse, even to the point where I wasn't sure I could make it through the night. I prayed with all my heart, asking God for some type of relief. Things continued to get worse, and I didn't know what to do. At one point while returning from the lavatory I felt like I was going to pass out, but being alone I knew I had to get back to my seat. Somehow I made it. As I sat there perspiring and breathing heavily, the thought came to me that I should quit complaining and express gratitude to God for the wonderful members and missionaries I had been with in India. As I bowed my head and offered up my sincere thanks, I began to feel a slight glimmer of peace. For the first time in what seemed forever, the spasms began to calm, and the need to retch began to fade a little. With even deeper gratitude I continued to thank the Lord for His love and goodness. I thought I should get some rest, as I was exhausted, but my mind would not allow me to relax. From nowhere, yet everywhere, I seemed to hear a soft voice say: "Look."

I looked out the window and saw myriads of stars in the cloudless sky. It was as though I could see and feel the power of God moving in His majesty through the immensity of space. I marveled at His greatness—His power—His order—His love—His goodness—and His infinite, endless creations. As I contemplated these truths, I felt another gentle command saying,

"Look." I sensed I was to look at the earth below, not just at the stars above.

I looked down but could only see darkness. My natural tendency was to look up again, for there I could clearly see an endless stream of bright, scintillating stars. Again I felt the gentle request: "Look." I knew I should look down again. I looked and looked, trying to see anything below, but still I could see only darkness. Our route put us somewhere near the Himalaya Mountains, flying across China at a very high altitude toward Hong Kong. Again and again I looked, straining to see something—anything. Suddenly I saw a small, dim light fading in and out. I concentrated on its location: *There it is, now a little brighter,* I thought. Then I saw another light—even smaller, but a definite light, and this one held quite still.

With excitement I looked more intensely and saw another light, then another. The harder I looked, the more lights I saw. Soon I saw many lights—some single, some in clusters. Were these small Chinese villages? My mind went back to the wonderful members and missionaries in India and the light coming from their faces. However, we were now over China, not India, and I knew there were precious few members in China right now. As my mind grappled with these thoughts, that same gentle voice or influence explained that there were many good people in China. In fact there were good people in every part of the world—Asia, the Islands, the Americas, and beyond—and if I looked long enough, hard enough, and with enough faith, I could see them.

I wanted to see and understand more. That same influence let me know that I could if I would, so, despite the fact that I was still not feeling well, I continued to look. I gained a deeper understanding that light, life, liberty, and love all come from God, and that the light of Christ, which is in each one of us (see Doctrine and Covenants 93:2), will guide us to Him as we respond to its promptings. Some refer to this light of Christ as conscience, while others refer to it in different terms, but it is the same. It has been and will be in all people from all cultures over all time (see Doctrine and Covenants 88:7–13).

Everyone has the gift of moral agency—the right to choose. Some people use their agency to move toward the light and increase in kindness and goodness and receive more light. Others use their agency to pursue selfish ends and move away from the light. Most of us do some of both, but we can always turn and move toward the light, even from deep degrees of darkness. As we change and live more in accord with God's laws—a process called repentance—we move toward the light, becoming brighter and brighter, and understanding more and more.

I learned that there are countless good people everywhere, and the more we look for the good (the light) in others, the more of it we will see. The light in everyone, no matter how faint, responds to the testimony of Christ, who is the source of all light. So we have a huge responsibility to bear fervent testimony of Him in both word and action. Indeed, He has commanded us: "Let your light so shine before men, that they may see your good works, and glorify your Father which is in heaven" (Matthew 5:16; see also verses 14–15).

As I thought more about light, I recalled the pleading of the brother of Jared: "O Lord . . . suffer not that [we] shall go forth across this raging deep in darkness . . . touch these stones . . . that they may shine forth in darkness . . . that we may have light while we shall cross the sea" (Ether 3:3–4).

In compassion, the Lord touched the stones, and they glowed. Similarly, He will help us increase the light in our lives if we will let Him. We need not travel through life in darkness.

The only way we can truly believe in Christ with sufficient faith to eventually be perfected in Him is to respond to His light within us. Jesus came to do the will of the Father, which includes drawing all men unto Him (see 3 Nephi 27:13–15; John 12:49).

Now I began to understand the Savior's statement, "That which is righteous cometh down from above, from the Father of lights" (Doctrine and Covenants 67:9).

As I pondered these truths, my mind went to Gethsemane on that darkest of nights. I sensed that when the Savior began His agonizing ordeal He gazed longingly at the stars above, with which He was intimately familiar and from whence He had come. Then He searched into the darkness all about Him through which He was passing and saw myriads of lights through that darkness. While enduring the cruel torment and pain of that terrible night, He comprehended and loved every single light—each person—throughout the universe.

I followed Him from the garden to the mock trial and cried out in pain at His scourging. I hung my head when those He had helped cried: "Crucify him—crucify him!" I saw Him lifted up on the cruel cross and suffering again. *How much more must He endure?* I wondered.

I saw Him suffering on the cross and, through unbearable pain, searching out His mother and making certain she would be cared for by John. I sensed Him looking beyond the milling, taunting mob and seeing women at wells, hungry crowds being fed, sightless men seeing, lifeless children arising, cleansed lepers leaping, and multitudes of halt, maimed, possessed, sin-bound, helpless souls being healed and freed and saved. Again He comprehended the light in every person from every age from everywhere over all time, and loved each one with such unfathomable love that His great heart swelled to its breaking point. Then, when He knew He had paid the full price so every light could be pulled through the darkness, He looked heavenward.

Instantly I heard a ripping sound and felt a blinding flash as a galactic thunderbolt split the darkness of all creation, and the Savior's humble words penetrated all eternity: "It is finished. . . . Father, into thy hands I commend my spirit" (John 19:30; Luke

23:46). He had done it! The cost in blood and tears and pain to satisfy justice and make this saving possible is incomprehensible to mortal man—but I know He did it! All I could do was weep and wonder and praise. I was so weak from witnessing these excruciating yet majestic scenes that there was only silent sobbing left in me.

Then through my tears I seemed to see a large stone begin to tremble and groan as it slowly moved. Suddenly there was a tremendous outpouring of light that seemed to encompass everything and everyone and everywhere. Darkness was replaced by light, death by life, despair by hope, and sorrow by joy. All existence seemed to breathe a smile. The Savior's love had triumphed! Now it was possible for each light to grow brighter and brighter so that each one could eventually become part of the celestial lights above—if they chose to continue in God. "That which is of God is light; and he that receiveth light, and continueth in God, receiveth more light; and that light groweth brighter and brighter until the perfect day" (Doctrine and Covenants 50:24).

I spent a long time expressing my deepest gratitude, but knew it was not adequate. I began to see how every living creature could shout hosannas forever: "And they rest not day and night, saying, Holy, holy, holy, Lord God Almighty, which was, and is, and is to come" (Revelation 4:8).

Gradually I became aware that the sky was becoming lighter and the stars were growing fainter. I didn't want to lose my friends the stars, nor the lights below with their unlimited potential. I pled with the Lord to let me stay in this element a little longer. Yet despite my plea, the stars were fading and we were landing. Again, I felt that gentle whisper, saying: "Look around you. Look—find—love—enlighten—testify—sacrifice—do all you can to help others come to Christ, and all will be well."

I knew that I had seen and heard and felt much more than I could then comprehend. However, I was given the assurance that over time, and as needed, these understandings would be opened a little here and a little there, for everything was indelibly etched on my soul. It was a glorious feeling.

As we landed, I realized that the last part of my flight had been much more glorious than the first part had been miserable. I was struck with the importance of the sequence I had just experienced: doing your duty, being humble and grateful (through illness or otherwise), then being willing to listen, then to look, then to see (with more than mortal eyes), then to feel, then to obey and help.

As we rolled to a stop, my body felt weak but my spirit felt strong. When I disembarked it seemed that the physical world around me hardly existed. I sort of floated off the plane, through Immigration and Customs, and toward my waiting ride. I felt like smiling and talking to everyone. I was surprised at how busy those around me seemed to be and how few smiled or even had time to talk—especially about the important things of eternity. It seemed strange.

Then I remembered that we are here to be tested—to learn, to obey, and thus to allow the light within us to shine brighter and brighter. I knew that all of us, including myself, must do better, no matter where we are or who we are with. If we do, I know that someone, somewhere will respond, and together we will grow and glow and eventually be able to partake of His full power and shine forth brilliantly forever.

Chapter 29

LOST IN MALAYSIA

Why are we sometimes so stubborn? I don't know, but I am sure we would be better off if we listened more intently to one another.

On our way to an assignment in Singapore, Jean and I went to Malaysia for a few days of R & R. We were met in Kuala Lumpur by a driver who took us up to Fraser's Hill in the highlands, about two and a half hours up a winding road. The last eight miles of this road are so steep and narrow that it can handle only one-way traffic. There is a gate at each end of this section of road, allowing traffic to go uphill for forty minutes on the odd hours and downhill on the even hours.

The only hotel available was old and rundown. Arriving there just before midnight, we made a couple of room changes before getting running water and other things that worked. But the next morning dawned clear and beautiful. It was cool in the highlands—a welcome relief from the oppressive heat of Hong Kong at that time of year.

Fraser's Hill is an old resort area where British settlers used to come to escape the summer heat. One of the things the area is famous for is its annual International Bird Race. Birders come from all over the world during the month of June to spot some of the huge variety of exotic birds that can be found there (around 270 species). The "race" is won by the team of three that identifies the most species of birds within a given time.

The surrounding hills were filled with all sorts of trails. Early in the morning we went on a beautiful trail and were back to the hotel by noon. As it did nearly every day, the mist rolled in and it rained for a couple of hours, then cleared up. We took another trail that afternoon, with even more beautiful vistas. The next morning we took yet another trail, returning by noon. Again it rained, this time longer and harder.

That afternoon I was anxious to try the two trails we hadn't taken. Jean was reluctant and wanted to wait until the next morning because it was now fairly late in the afternoon. I should have listened to her, but I didn't. Being a good sport, Jean came along. The first trail was well marked and so beautiful that when we came to the second one I was excited to try it also. Jean wanted to go back, but, judging from the map, it appeared the remaining

One of the trails at Fraser's Hill, Malaysia.

trail wasn't very long. So, against Jean's intuition and at my urging, off we went.

That was when the real adventure began. We were the only ones on the trail, and, according to the map, it ended at a small cabin, but instead it just kept going and going. We got deeper and deeper into the jungle/forest. The trail was very narrow in places along the steep mountainside—we were grateful that someone had put ropes to hold onto in the steepest places. It was muddy and wet and slippery and dangerous. Surely we must be near the end by now.

Suddenly, Jean cried out. Something was biting her foot. It was a leech! We pulled it off and continued on. We were sure we were more than halfway along the trail, so it would be longer and more dangerous to turn back than to just go on. The trail got worse and the light got dimmer. Both of us were in a bit of a panic by now. We could barely make out the trail ahead. We stopped and prayed, asking for protection and enough light to make it off the steep, treacherous mountain.

We pressed forward. I was in the lead, and didn't dare mention the snakes that often scurried out of my way. It was so dark and slippery now that we hardly dared move. One false step and one of us could sprain an ankle or break a leg or fall down the hill. We both knew we were in trouble, and the sting of unseen leeches didn't help matters.

Then, just as the sun dipped below the mountain, bringing darkness to the forest, we saw some lights in the distance. "Thank goodness," I thought, "we are close to the end." We parted some bushes to see if we could identify the lights and how to get to them. As we did, we heard the sound of distant voices. My hopes were raised—if we could hear them, surely they could hear us!

I decided to yell for help. I yelled and yelled, but to no effect; the chatter, which faded in and out, continued at about the same level. Our situation was desperate. Why hadn't I listened to Jean?

We took a few steps, but slipped and fell with nearly every step. It simply wasn't worth the risk. Jean pled with me not to move more, for if I fell and broke a leg, she could not carry me.

We prayed again. I felt a deep rebuke for not having listened to my wife. Now I had gotten us both into a terrible situation. We felt our way to some nearby rocks and sat on them. By now we both felt multiple stings from leeches, and lightning and thunder were coming toward us. Soon it would start raining, and we were still high on this steep hill. It was dangerous either to move or not to move. What could we do?

I asked Jean to join with me, and we yelled as loudly as we could, but our efforts to attract the attention of the distant voices seemed in vain. Maybe if we moved a little closer to the lights it might help. As soon as we tried, we started slipping down a steep slope and realized that there was a deep ravine between us and the lights. I tried to think of every option, and the safest one seemed to be to just sit down and wait through the night until it got light enough to see the trail.

Just as I was getting reconciled to this, I thought of the leeches and the snakes and the rain and wondered if there weren't some other alternative. We prayed as hard and sincerely as we knew how. It was now very dark and late and we were lost and in deep trouble in the steep, slippery mountains of Malaysia. I was totally subdued, and vowed that I would never override my wife's intuition again. I held Jean's hand, told her how sorry I was and how much I loved her, and asked for her forgiveness. Of course, she was an angel and said to forget about it. That is easier said than done.

We agreed that I would yell once more, and if it didn't raise anyone, we would just sit where we were through the night, pick off as many leeches as we could, and count our blessings. As I got up to yell for help once more, I felt impressed to cup my hands at my mouth, like a mini-megaphone, and with all my energy make one long, loud cry of the single word "H—e—e—l—l—p—p," holding it for as long as I could. At the end of that long distress cry, we heard the distant mumble of voices change a little. I cried out again, as long and loud as I could. There was a response, but not in English.

I called out once more. We waited and waited. Nothing. I yelled again. Then came some of the most reassuring words either of us have ever heard: "Okay. Okay. Stay there. We come."

Soon tiny lights from a couple of flashlights began to move across the valley. But they seemed to be going away from us! We yelled again, "Over here!"

"Okay. Okay. Stay there. We come."

We watched the lights go far to our left, then eventually come up a long, steep trail to our left. Seldom have either of us seen a more welcome sight than those five young men—one Indian, one Chinese, and three Malays—coming up the muddy trail with flashlights in hand. They were workers at a nearby hotel, and only the Indian spoke English. As they helped us down that treacherous mountainside, their melodic voices soothed our frazzled nerves. Even with their solicitous guiding we slid and slipped several times, banging against rocks and scraping against roots and limbs. Gratefully, within thirty minutes or so, we were off the mountain and back to a paved road.

Our new friends arranged for a taxi to take us up to the medical "Klinik" in town. We gave them what money we had and told Bala, the one who spoke English, to thank the others and let them know that God would bless them for their help. The taxi driver was anxious to leave, and our friends said they had to get back to work, so we parted. By the time we got to the town, the medical "Klinik" was closed, so the driver took us to our hotel. When we got to our room, we collapsed in gratitude and prayer.

We then felt we must remove the leeches. The only way we knew to do that was to pull them off. We learned the next day that if we had put a little salt on them, the leeches would have died and fallen off without leaving bleeding holes. We also later realized that we had somehow missed getting special stockings that leeches can't penetrate. By the time we got through ridding ourselves of the dozens of leeches, it was two o'clock in the morning and the bathroom floor was pooled with blood. Fortunately, the floor in the bathroom was tile and had a floor drain. Jean started laughing and said, "Aren't we having fun? This is just like washing out all those dirty diapers and bedding late at night in Idaho Falls, that you wrote about."*

I don't know if it was the laughter, the trauma, the gratitude, the memories, or what, but neither of us could sleep, even though we were physically and emotionally exhausted. I suppose we both realized how close we had come to a possible catastrophe, or at the least to spending a miserable night lost on a Malaysian mountain.

In the final analysis, despite my foolishness, the Lord heard and answered our prayers. The lights stayed on long enough for some humble workers to come and get us safely back. Jean was wonderful through the whole thing. I'm sure it was the purity of her heart, more than anything, that brought those young men with their lights, and help, and knowledge of the trail.

I suppose this experience is similar to many of the problems we bring upon ourselves in life. We could spare ourselves a lot of trouble if we would prepare better, get better information, and listen more intently to one another and to the Spirit (which often speaks through our spouses). Yet, thankfully and humbly, I know that when we are in trouble, when we are lost and don't know the way, when darkness overtakes us and the stings of life are painful, the Lord is there and help is available, anytime, anywhere.

---

*See *The Fire of Faith*, p. 246.

Chapter 30

PROFESSOR PHAN

When Jean and I first visited Vietnam, we took with us a letter of introduction from an American doctor to a Doctor Phan in Hanoi. These two doctors had worked together for some time under the banner of "Operation Smile." Through their mutual efforts to help children with cleft palates, they had become good friends, first professionally, then personally.

Doctor Phan received us kindly, spoke fondly of his American doctor friend, and assured us he would help us as much as he could. We found that he was known by several titles—Doctor, General, Professor—but he preferred to be addressed as Professor Phan because he saw himself mostly as a teacher helping others learn how to heal those in need. Over the next several years, whenever we went to Vietnam, we visited him and our friendship grew.

Professor Phan was born and raised in Vietnam, studied medicine abroad, returned to Vietnam, married, and had three daughters. He saw himself as a Vietnamese patriot and fought to rid his homeland of outside influences, be they Chinese, French, or American. He served his country as a doctor in the military and rose to the rank of general. He was extremely competent and soon held the position in Vietnam equivalent to that of the U.S. Surgeon General.

He had a kind nature and used his skills to save lives wherever he could. During the war with America, he insisted on personally treating captured American airmen who had been injured when their planes were shot down. He saved the lives of many American pilots who under other circumstances would not have survived. I once asked him how he felt about treating soldiers who had just bombed his hometown of Hanoi. He simply said, "They were injured and I could help, so I did. After all, they were only boys doing their duty as assigned by their superiors. I hold nothing against them personally. I hope the Americans treated injured North Vietnamese military prisoners with the same humanity." He told me that his father had been killed by the French and his brother by the Americans, but war was war. He did not hold a grudge against people fighting for what they believed.

After the war ended, he used his influence to develop a private surgical clinic for treating young people, especially those born with cleft palates. (Vietnam has a high incidence of this birth defect.) Professor Phan and others at his clinic were able to repair this defect in many, allowing them to function well and overcome what otherwise might be a lifetime of living in the shadows or on the margins of society. It was in connection with this clinic that Professor Phan met his LDS doctor friend, through whom the Church became aware of and supported Professor Phan's efforts by sending medical equipment and several humanitarian missionary couples to Vietnam. Those missionaries have taught English to medical students and helped in various other ways at hospitals, orphanages, and colleges.

Professor Phan provided valuable assistance to the Church on several occasions by arranging meetings for us with government officials, enabling us to work out challenges that constantly arose

Professor-Doctor Phan.

regarding visas, rental of facilities, and authorization for Church meetings. He always dealt with us and others with honesty and integrity. He never asked for money. How wonderful it was to have an honest and influential friend in a country where the Church was barely getting started. What a great amount of good one talented, trusted, honest, and well-placed individual can do! How I admired his attitude and desire to help others.

After the Hong Kong Temple dedication in 1996, we had the privilege of flying with President and Sister Gordon B. Hinckley and a few others to Cambodia and Vietnam. Early one morning on the banks of the Mekong River, President Hinckley dedicated the land of Cambodia for the preaching of the gospel. Afterwards, we flew to Ho Chi Minh City (formerly Saigon), Vietnam, where we held a meeting with some expatriate Church members and a few Vietnamese Latter-day Saints who had joined the Church years ago and had stayed in Vietnam during the tumultuous years of war and rebuilding. We climbed to the roof level of the Caravelle Hotel, where President Hinckley reminisced about those hectic war days. What a contrast to the calm and peace now!

We next flew to Hanoi, where we were met at the airport by Professor Phan and three other government officials. They gave President and Sister Hinckley beautiful flowers and expressed their deep appreciation for the humanitarian aid given to their

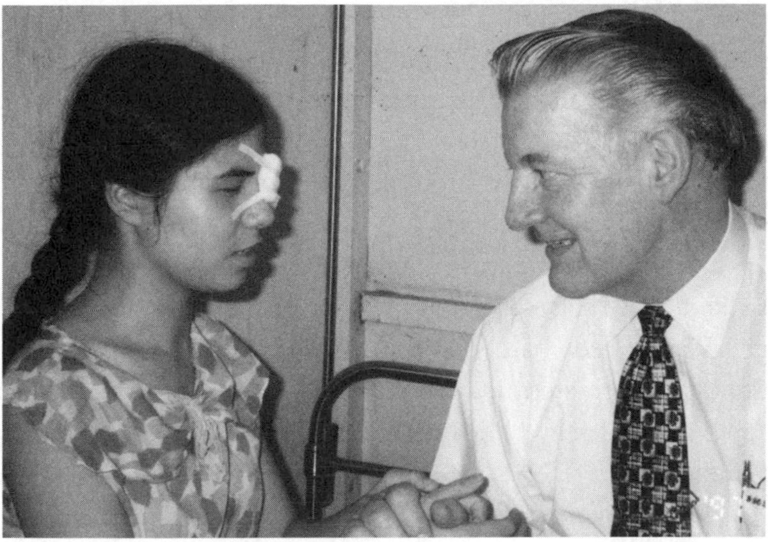

John with a Vietnamese girl whose eye problem we were able to help.

country. They appreciated everything, but specifically mentioned the wonderful couples who donated many hours in teaching English to medical students. President Hinckley thanked Professor Phan for his good life and his help to the Church and assured him that we would continue to help alleviate suffering in his country.

That afternoon we went to one of the Saints' homes and held a meeting with the few members (mostly expatriates) living in Hanoi. In this unusual and intimate setting, the Spirit was strong. President Hinckley spoke and bore a marvelous testimony. What a wonderful experience to feel the prophet's personal love for the people of Vietnam! There were many tears of gratitude as that small group quietly left that home.

A few months after this visit, I received a call from Hanoi, stating that Professor Phan was very ill. Things didn't look good, and he wondered if we could come and give him a blessing. I felt impressed to drop everything and go immediately to Hanoi. We thought we had made the proper arrangements, but Jean and I still had difficulty getting into the carefully guarded military hospital where Professor Phan was being treated. Those in charge might have felt uneasy about an American Christian religious leader visiting a decorated North Vietnamese general. Even with the help of his daughter, it took a while to get through the guards and into her father's room.

Entering his room was a somber yet beautiful occasion. There lay Professor Phan—this icon of North Vietnamese history—in pain, jaundiced, barely able to move, but still smiling. He expressed deep gratitude for our visit and said he would really appreciate a blessing. I knew God would look with favor on that request.

Here lay a former North Vietnamese military general, a non-Christian, a "communist," a nationalist dedicated to expelling from his country those whom he perceived as foreign intruders. Here lay a brilliant doctor of medicine who, despite the fact that his father and brother had been killed by foreigners, still carried compassion in his heart for everyone, including foreigners. He had treated thousands of wounded combatants, including dozens of downed American pilots, with skill and kindness. Only God knows the lives he saved and the people—especially children—he helped.

Here lay a man who felt a unity of purpose and a kindred spirit with a fellow doctor involved in the same work who happened to be a Mormon stake president. He extended that feeling to other members of the Church. He appreciated and assisted all those who labored to relieve the suffering of his people. He recognized the value of donated time, expertise, and equipment, whether to close cleft palates, fit man-made limbs to the limbless, or teach English to doctors so they could better understand advanced medical literature. Here lay a man who against opposition championed the goodness of the Church and its members. With his help, the Church was able to stay in Vietnam during troubled times when otherwise it may have had virtually no standing or presence.

Yes, here lay Professor Phan, eaten by cancer, in pain, yet still expressing gratitude. His goodness and faith flooded my heart. Of course he hoped to live, but realizing that he may not, he had obtained promises from three of his colleagues to carry on the work of his surgical clinic and to continue helping the Church in Vietnam.

As he had requested in faith believing, I gave him a blessing. The whole room was filled with goodness and light. In the blessing he was given the assurance that he had a Father in Heaven who knew and loved him and who was pleased with the goodness of his heart and his life. I came to understand more deeply than ever that God loves all of His children and is pleased when they help one another.

When the blessing ended Dr. Phan was very quiet. Then he whispered, "Thank you. I understand. I know I am going back to a loving Father. I love you and appreciate your help to me and to my people. Thanks for the blessing. Would you bless my daughters also?"

I promised I would as I whispered to him, "Be at peace—all will be well."

There were no dry eyes in the room. His daughter, a beautiful married woman in her mid-thirties, asked if she could receive a blessing right then. I gave her a blessing, and a similar beautiful experience ensued. Some of the understandings received were so sacred it was as if we were in a different dimension of time and space. I know the Lord was pleased with this fine woman and her willingness to put off the call of business (she was president of a large insurance company in Hanoi) to spend her valuable time in caring for her father.

When this blessing concluded, I looked deeply into her eyes and asked, "Do you have any Christian background or understanding?"

"No," she replied, "but now I believe in God."

I knew she meant it. I asked if she understood who Jesus was and what He did for us.

"No," she said, "except I know He loves me and wants to help me."

Our stay had extended to a point where the hospital attendants, who had left temporarily, returned. With their return our privacy evaporated, but the aura of goodness lingered. Still, I felt impressed to teach this wonderful woman and her father how to pray. I explained that they should address their Father in Heaven (in whom they now believed), thank Him for His blessings, ask for His help, and then close in the name of Jesus Christ (who they knew loved them). When I finished, I asked if they understood and would pray accordingly. "Yes," they said. "Yes, we will."

We had a difficult time parting. Finally, after several heartfelt good-byes, Jean and I were led away by another doctor to the busy outside world of Hanoi. We left more determined than ever to purify our hearts, help others more sincerely, and please God more fully.

Professor Phan died a few weeks later.

I know that greatness of soul, purity of purpose, and helpfulness of heart can be found in all parts of the world. I know the kingdom of God will move forward in Vietnam, in Asia, and throughout the whole world. God says it will happen, and it will! We may have temporary setbacks, but the overall direction is sure. I know God has His noble souls planted, placed, and prepared in all parts of the world and on both sides of the veil. I hope to be humble enough, loving enough, courageous enough, patient enough, and faithful enough to recognize them.

PART TWO

On our next trip to Hanoi after Professor Phan's death, his daughter who had been with us in the hospital hosted us at a lovely lunch. She again expressed her appreciation for the blessing and for our help to her family. We asked how we could meet her other two sisters. She explained that one lived in the United States and the other was a busy surgeon in Hanoi. She called and found that the sister in Hanoi was in surgery at a nearby hospital but was anxious to see us. She had left word that if we could come to the hospital, she would arrange to see us between operations.

Upon arriving at the hospital, we were taken through some interesting back halls and stairways to a small room. Soon a beautiful lady doctor, still in her surgical clothing, entered. She was all smiles and delighted to see us. We visited for a while.

We talked about the passing of her father. I told her the same things I had told her sister—that her father's spirit is alive and well and aware of more things now than when he was in this life. I explained about God our Father and about Jesus our Savior,

Mission President and Sister White, Professor Phan's daughter, Jean and John.

about prayer (which she promised to try), about body and spirit, about growth and forgiveness, and about the resurrection.

She drank it all in without ever averting her eyes. She seemed to be looking right through me. When I finished, she started to cry and asked, "Do you really believe these things?" I was taken aback a little and assured her that I not only believed them, I knew them to be true. She was visibly shaken. With a penetrating gaze she said, "Oh, how I want to believe that. Oh, how I wish I could believe that. Help me so I can."

We tried to help her in every way we could. We taught from the scriptures and testified from our hearts. During our visit she requested and received a blessing much like the one I had given her sister. It was a beautiful experience. When we finished, she thanked us profusely and said again that she would give anything to believe the things I had explained. I promised her she could believe them if she wanted to strongly enough and would plant and nurture the seed of faith in her heart. She promised she would sincerely try. We left, and she returned to her operating room to continue her work in assisting in the healing of bodies. We hoped we had somehow assisted in healing her soul.

During that visit I was shown again what is truly valuable. Cars, clothes, houses, and other physical trappings mean virtually nothing in the long run. Even secular education, fame, fortune, good looks, or physical prowess are of little value by themselves. What is of inestimable value is to believe, to have faith in God and in the basic truths of eternity: God is our Father. He loves us. Jesus is our Savior and loves us. The Holy Ghost testifies to us and gives us assurances that there is life after death, there is a resurrection, there is a final judgment. Forgiveness, love, and kindness are real and eternal. I know this knowledge is of most value and is available to anyone who truly desires it.

I will always remember that beautiful young doctor as she fervently pled: "Oh, how I want to believe. How I wish I could believe. Help me to believe." Nothing else at that moment was as valuable to her as to be able to believe the things she had just been taught. She would have given most anything to have that faith. I wonder, in contrast, how many of us allow our precious testimonies of these truths to lie dormant or even decay.

Oh, how I hope we will never take for granted the basic ability to believe—the gift of faith, which is so liberally given to us. It is of more value than we can comprehend. Its value becomes more evident when we meet those who, for whatever reason, don't seem to be able to believe, especially when such people desperately want to believe.

We were given the address of Professor Phan's youngest daughter, who lived in the Seattle, Washington, area with her husband. After we returned from Hong Kong and were again living in Bountiful, I received a conference assignment in the Seattle area, and while there I contacted this daughter. She was anxious to visit with me. My sister and brother-in-law who lived in the area drove me to her lovely home, where we were warmly welcomed. We had a wonderful visit with her and her husband. I was able to fulfill her father's request that all three of his daughters receive a priesthood blessing. This daughter shared with us a video of her father's funeral service, which she and her husband had attended in Hanoi. The funeral was a fascinating combination of government, military, and Buddhist pageantry. We also detected a hint of Christianity.

I am grateful for the life of Professor Phan. His humility, his good heart, and his willingness to help others will become a great blessing for many people. Anyone, anytime, anywhere can be of assistance to God in bringing blessings into the lives of His children. Professor Phan is one of those. I know there is a place reserved and a mission for him to fulfill in the realms above. I am certain God is pleased with his life.

Chapter 31

A VISIT WITH A GENERAL

Cambodia had always been a place of mystery and intrigue to me. I was excited but a little apprehensive as I prepared for my first visit there. Largely through the help of a well-educated Cambodian member who had joined the Church in Thailand, the Cambodian government had recently given recognition to the Church. We quickly sent a missionary couple and four young elders to the capital, Phnom Penh, to start the work. Although Phnom Penh was considered safe, the Khmer Rouge guerrillas were still a threat in the countryside, and the political situation was somewhat unstable.

International commerce was just restarting in Cambodia after many years of war and unrest, so our small plane from Hong Kong was not very full. The flight that lasted several hours seemed much longer because of my anxiety. At last, the flat, flooded fields of Cambodia came into view. Feelings of wonder and intrigue and thoughts of wars past and recent went through my mind. I felt great responsibility for the missionaries and wanted to be certain that they were safe and that the work of the Lord was moving forward in this land so new to the gospel.

We landed at an old military airport near Phnom Penh and taxied a long way over very bumpy concrete. We finally stopped in front of a set of ramshackle buildings. The plane's door opened, and heavy, hot air rushed in.

As I started down the stairs, I noticed dozens of young boys in uniforms "playing" with their military rifles. There seemed to be a general lack of order. Some soldiers pointed for us to go to a certain building, which turned out to be the Immigration area. The process of getting into the country was chaotic, and I was filled with trepidation as soldier after soldier ordered us to fill out this form or that one, requested money for processing fees, and pointed for us to go here or there. After a long, tense time, I finally cleared Immigration. The people outside seemed no more disciplined than the soldiers inside, but at least they weren't carrying guns! It was a relief to see a neatly dressed missionary couple waiting for me.

It was late afternoon when we reached the rented home where the couple and the four elders were staying. It was a pleasant home, and their needs seemed to be met. I was happy to learn that the four young elders spoke excellent Cambodian. They had served the first part of their missions in California among Cambodian refugees.

After a light meal we started our missionary meeting. The missionaries, a few Cambodian members, and myself were present. We had just finished our song and prayer when the phone rang. A Cambodian member who helped the missionaries with housework answered it. After listening for a moment she turned pale, dropped the phone, and gathered her things to leave.

"What is it?" asked one of the elders as he picked up the phone.

"It's from an army general. He said we have a high-ranking Church official here and he wants to come talk to him."

The elder with the phone then turned to me and asked how he should reply. I could tell that those in the room were uneasy, even frightened. However, a strong impression came to me, and I said, "Tell him to come. Tell him we will be here for the next two hours and we will be happy to meet with him."

I wasn't entirely calm, but I wasn't overly concerned either. I had prayed a good deal about this trip, the missionaries, and the work in Cambodia. Now that I was here meeting with the missionaries, I knew that the Lord, who was in charge, would give me direction.

As we waited for our guest to arrive, the level of our apprehension increased. One by one the few Cambodian members and investigators who were present quietly slipped away. They were not taking any chances! The rest of us didn't know what to expect, but since we had promised to meet with the general, we continued praying and waiting.

Soon a convoy of army vehicles drove up. In the front was a jeep with a mounted machine gun. As the convoy stopped, several smartly dressed soldiers jumped down and quickly positioned themselves strategically around the rented home. One soldier opened the door of a car and, amidst the click of heels and the snap of salutes, the general stepped out and came to our front door accompanied by two aides.

I met them at the door and welcomed them in. The interior of the house was mostly bare, except for two couches facing each other with two chairs on either end. I invited the general and his aides to sit on one couch while two of the missionaries and I sat on the couch facing them. The other two missionaries sat on the chairs on one end, and the couple sat on the chairs on the other end.

It was a warm evening, so we offered them some lemonade. I was relieved when the general smiled and nodded yes to our offer.

We sat for several awkward minutes, sipping lemonade and sizing each other up. I wasn't sure what to expect.

Finally the general spoke to me through his interpreter. He welcomed us to Cambodia and wanted to know more about our plans. I was having difficulty understanding his interpreter, but the missionary beside me followed the general's Cambodian and clarified several points. The general smiled and in Cambodian asked the elder how well he understood the language. The elder responded that he understood it well. The general turned to his aide and said he would use the elder to interpret for him. His aide seemed relieved.

The general asked about our beliefs and what we hoped to accomplish in Cambodia. I explained our purpose and how we hoped to help the Cambodian people by teaching eternal truths such as the Fatherhood of God and the brotherhood of man. I explained the role of the missionaries in this process and mentioned that they also taught English classes. He smiled approvingly. I then felt impressed to explain in some detail about the Book of Mormon. I reviewed what it was, what it taught, and presented a copy to him. He graciously accepted it. When I finished, the general explained that he was Buddhist but felt pleased with what he had heard.

He was very formal and sat with rigid military bearing. I could tell he was thinking. Suddenly, he turned even more serious, looked me straight in the eye, and said: "I want you to know that I will protect your boys. You don't need to worry. No harm will come to them. I feel good about what you plan to do. Welcome to Cambodia."

He looked at each of the four young elders and seemed to get a faraway look in his eyes. He continued, "These are fine boys. I feel good about them being here. It is much better to sit down and use words and books to discuss our differences rather than guns and bullets.

"During the war many of your young American boys were killed here. I felt sorry for them. They were just boys, much like these boys here tonight. Let's have no more shooting. Let's use words and books to talk about our different ideas. I like these boys; I will protect them. You have my word. Don't worry about them."

It was as though he was reading my mind and addressing my concern. I thanked him for his promise and told him I trusted him. I assured him the missionaries were "good boys." When I finished, he stood up and gave a command, and his aides scurried to get properly positioned at his side. He said he must leave now. I extended my hand, which he took in a firm handshake. Again he said sincerely, "Don't worry. I'll protect them; they will be all right. I like these boys. Books and words are much better than guns and bullets."

He turned and left. There was more clicking of heels, loading of cars, and roaring of engines, and soon the military convoy moved back into the night from whence it had come.

I looked at those around me. Their faces showed a combination of disbelief and delight. Restrained smiles appeared and the built-up tension began to melt. I suggested we close our missionary meeting with a prayer of thanksgiving and continue in the morning. Everyone agreed.

As I offered that closing prayer, I knew I had received the answer I had so earnestly sought. I knew the direction the Lord wanted us to take in Cambodia. Yes, there would be challenges, but "our boys" would be safe. The work would grow. The Lord had accepted the sacrifices of many on both sides of the veil. I knew His work would move forward in Cambodia.

We all slept well that night.

POSTSCRIPT

About two years later, on May 29, 1996, Jean and I had the privilege of accompanying President and Sister Hinckley and a few others as the prophet officially dedicated the land of Cambodia for the preaching of the gospel. On July 1, 1997, the Cambodian Mission was created. Since then the Church has grown and most everything else in Cambodia has improved. About ten years after that first "visit with a general," there were three districts, nearly 7,000 members, several chapels, and many missionaries, both local and from other countries. The Lord's work continues to grow in Cambodia. The missionaries and welfare service couples have been safe.

On one of our last trips to Cambodia, before leaving our assignment in Hong Kong, Jean and I visited the infamous "Killing Fields." It is estimated that possibly up to 20 percent of the population of Cambodia was killed during the Pol Pot genocide years. As we approached those fields, Jean suddenly asked

The Grobergs, Wirthlins, President and Sister Hinckley, and missionaries at the dedication of Cambodia for preaching the gospel.

A Young Women's choir in Phnom Penh, Cambodia.

the driver to stop for a moment. She got out her camera and took a picture of some beautiful water lilies growing in a tiny, muddy pond in front of a humble abode. It was a poignant scene showing the triumph of truth, goodness, and beauty over travesty, greed, and debauchery—a beautiful illustration of the Savior's words: "Consider the lilies of the field . . ." (Matthew 6:28).*

As I have contemplated the message of this precious photo, I have been struck with the truth that from death, God can and does bring life. Even with so much suffering and such great tragedy among the distressed people of Cambodia, the Lord has heard the cries of the innocent and has blessed them and their country with the gospel. Present-day Cambodian members of the Church are now able to help their ancestors in ways never before imagined. Many who died in sorrow now rejoice as sacred ordinances are performed in their behalf.

I have had no further contact with that general, but he has kept his promise. How important it is that we heed the prompt-

---

*The photograph appears on the back cover of this book.

ings of the Spirit and are always thoughtful of others! We do not know how the Lord may use them in advancing His cause. As I think back on that rather frightening time, I realize more than ever how the Lord can, and does, use anyone, anytime, anywhere—even a Cambodian general—to move His work forward.

I have witnessed, time and time again, great good accomplished to and through a large variety of God's children. I know that every one of us is capable of giving and receiving marvelous blessings. There is no limit to the good that can be achieved when we sincerely strive to do what is right. I know that all of us as God's children are blessed when we strive to live up to the potential that is within us. Whether we be a mechanic, student, doctor, decorated war hero, or someone still trying to find the path in this life, God's love and blessings are available to us all—anytime, anywhere.

Chapter 32

ONE ETERNAL ROUND

After going anytime, anywhere in all the world, for thirty consecutive years, we were called by President Gordon B. Hinckley to return to Idaho and serve as president and matron of the Idaho Falls Temple. It had never occurred to us that going anywhere might someday mean going back to Idaho Falls. But here it was: We were going home—back to where I was born and raised, back to where I left as a young missionary to Tonga, back to where Jean and I began our family and a business, back to where nine of our eleven children were born, and back to where we left to fulfill the call received from President Spencer W. Kimball to serve anytime and anywhere as a General Authority.

Going home! What powerful and profound emotions that simple phrase evokes! Why? Because God has planted deep within each of us an inner feeling that, like a celestial homing device, reminds us that our earthly home is not our final home—that we have come from a heavenly home where we were loved and nurtured and to where we long to return. Is it any wonder that the phrase "going home" has been the subject of or inspiration behind much of the greatest music composed, literature written, sermons delivered, and, indeed, lives lived?

After living in our Hong Kong "high rise home" for four years we were welcomed back to our Bountiful "home home."

This universal feeling is manifest in the lives of people from wildly different cultures, languages, and circumstances. All seem to have encoded in their very makeup something that regularly draws them to a place they call home.

Our loving Heavenly Father wants all of His children to return safely home and has given us a plan to accomplish this. It is called the great plan of happiness, or the gospel of Jesus Christ. It is the foundation of all that is lastingly meaningful in life because it alone correctly and completely answers life's great questions: Where did we come from? Why are we here? Where are we going after this life?

Only when we find and accept this plan, with the Savior at the center, can we move onto the path that will bring us safely home to God who gave us life. Therefore, this plan must be explained to everyone (either here or hereafter) in a way they can understand and feel its importance. Living, teaching, and testifying of that plan is the burden of the scriptures and the prophets, and the individual responsibility of all who come to understand it. We are partners with God in this great endeavor.

In our family's efforts to share the gospel plan, we have moved about the world and met and loved a wide variety of people: humble Chinese farmers with immaculate garden plots, smiling Mongolian herdsmen roaming over vast deserts, loving Polynesian fishermen sailing among small islands, hardworking Argentine ranchers riding through endless pampas, sophisticated professionals working in Hong Kong high-rises, to name but a few. God loves them all—right where they are—and wants them to hear, accept, and live the gospel and return safely home!

As I reflected on this truth, I remembered a train ride through central Mongolia where I looked through a frosted window and saw a loving family who needed the gospel. I recalled many individuals and families who miraculously found and lived the gospel in the islands of the Pacific, in the Andes Mountains, and many other places. I remembered being in a plane high above China where I saw lights representing many good people waiting to hear the gospel so they could know who they really are, what their destiny actually is, and what this yearning for home truly means.

As I reviewed our experiences from all over the world in the light of our new assignment, I was impressed with how frequently the thread of temple work had appeared in the fabric of those events. It was clear that as we learn and live His plan, temples and temple work come naturally. We all have two homes—one on this earth and one in heaven. One of our innermost desires, whether we presently comprehend it or not, is to make our home on earth like our home in heaven and then bring that home on earth with us to heaven. This can be done through temple ordinances.

I began to think more deeply about home, parents, temples, visions of possibilities, and the *power* and *pull* of families from all over the world and beyond. I thought of my own family, as well as other families. Our unanticipated call to return to Idaho Falls had evoked much the same rush of emotion and reflection that I experienced at the time of our unanticipated call to leave Idaho Falls. As my heart and mind raced, my thoughts kept returning to my parents. Both had lived long lives of faithful service to their family, the Church, and the community of Idaho Falls. Both had passed away within the previous year—Mom at 96 and Dad just weeks shy of 99 years of age.

One of the Brethren, aware of my new temple calling and the recent passing of my parents (and probably sensing the state of my emotions), reassuringly commented, "If anyone is entitled to walk the halls of the Idaho Falls Temple, it is your mom and dad." Something in his comment caused my feelings and thoughts to center more directly on families. I recognized order and design in what might have seemed random or coincidental occurrences.

Isn't the Lord's timing amazing? When President Spencer W. Kimball called us to leave Idaho Falls, he called Dad and Mom to stay in Idaho Falls and preside over the temple for five years. Now, thirty years later, when the Lord called Mom and Dad to leave Idaho Falls and return to their heavenly home, President Gordon B. Hinckley called us to return to Idaho Falls and follow in their footsteps in the temple.

My parents had stayed in Idaho Falls their entire married life of nearly 74 years, while Jean and I had "gone everywhere and done everything," so to speak. I realized, however, that there was no difference in either of our opportunities to learn, love, serve, and experience the peace and joy that come from following God's plan. The same is true for all of us. Everything we need in order to find and follow God's laws is available regardless of where we live or how far we travel. Remember, our Savior stayed pretty close to home during His earthly sojourn. It is our attitude and our desires, not our circumstances or our background, that make the difference.

As an example: Mom was raised in a large and prominent family in Provo, Utah. One grandfather had been mayor of Provo and the other one president of BYU. Her parents lived to an old age. By contrast, Dad was born in Idaho Falls but orphaned at age three when his mother died in childbirth and his father died a year later of tuberculosis. His only memory of either of his

Delbert V. and Jennie H. Groberg with John and Jean Groberg behind them. Also Delbert's parents and Grandmother Brunt shown above. This picture was taken from the site of the old family home.

parents was being lifted up to see his father on his deathbed. He remembered his father coughing, then smiling, looking into his eyes, rubbing his arm, and saying, "Delbert, be a good boy." It wasn't much, but it was enough!

Dad and his older brother were raised by an aunt and uncle on a farm in Utah, while his little sister was raised by their widowed grandmother in Idaho Falls. As a youth, Dad loved to return to Idaho Falls from the farm in Utah to see his Grandma Brunt and his little sister. On one such visit near the end of his grandma's life, something special happened. She walked with him across the street to the banks of the Snake River and reverently told him that one day a temple of the Lord would stand there. He knew she was a faithful woman and never doubted her inspiration.*

After Dad's mission, he and Mom met at BYU and, despite their differing backgrounds, fell in love, married in the Salt Lake Temple, and moved to Idaho Falls in 1930. As a young father and struggling businessman, Dad felt prompted to research the ownership of the sandy, seemingly worthless vacant lots by the river. He knew that his Grandma Brunt had seen a temple rising skyward from the river's edge. While he kept his grandmother's words to himself, he felt impelled to do something to help. When President Heber J. Grant announced the Church's intention to build a temple in Idaho, a local committee of Church and civic leaders asked Dad to identify some property to offer to the Church. When he told the committee he had already done so, they purchased the land and offered it to the Church. The Church accepted the site, and within a few years a gleaming white temple stood on the banks of the river across the street from their old family home, right where his grandmother had seen it.

Imagine the feelings of joy and fulfillment this temple brought to faithful families on both sides of the veil. I often think of the love and support that connected the family when Dad was called to serve as temple president. My own feelings on receiving this same call are full of profound love and gratitude for those who have gone before. We should all sense and respond to the *power* and *pull* of faithful people in our own families and heritage. It is real and strong and continues forever. Remember, life is eternal,

*See *The Fire of Faith,* chapter 12, "Don't Even Think of Complaining."

so all of us will eventually be with those who have loved and tried to help us.

We are all entitled to envision our life and our family as it can be. Think of the value of patriarchal blessings in this regard. Pay the price to get the vision, then pay the price to fulfill it. Great joy will surely come. I know God will help us in this endeavor. Don't worry too much if mistakes are made in your family. Try to learn from them and do better the next time, and always, always give an abundance of love and confidence.

Because of my parents' love for each other and their fervent testimonies of the gospel, my ten siblings and I (all born in Idaho Falls) always felt loved and secure. There were mistakes, challenges, discipline, and even occasional raised voices in our home, but as I think back on those growing-up years, my memory is mainly of the love and goodness I felt. I wonder if, when our mortal life is over and we look back on our earthly experiences, it won't be somewhat the same. Despite the rough times, we will remember mostly the positive times and the good people who loved, helped, and had confidence in us. We should do what we can to provide those positive experiences for those we love.

Some may feel that they don't have a chance for such joy because their parents are uneducated, poverty-stricken, or even unrighteous. Others may feel they "have it made" because of their high-pedigreed heritage. Both are wrong. In every case we must individually study and work hard to gain our own testimonies and vision of our potential. We all know good parents who weep over wayward children, or righteous children who pray over prodigal parents. As we keep living God's commandments, regardless of the challenges we may face, with His help we will eventually achieve our goal.

We may not have much control over what kind of parents we come to, but we do have control over what kind of parents we will be. Abraham became the "father of the faithful" despite his father's idolatry. As we choose to obey God, we can become true Israelites and receive the blessings of Abraham, Isaac, and Jacob. In that sense it is possible for all of us to have great parents (see Abraham 2:10).

Traveling and living among many people in many places, we have learned conclusively that there are good people everywhere. We know God loves them and is guiding them to find and live His great plan of happiness, which includes His temple. Where and how His children get on that road can be as varied as the personalities and circumstances that exist on earth. How grateful we are to know firsthand that people from every conceivable background are moving in the right direction! They often start with tiny steps, sometimes sliding back, but eventually taking larger steps forward. As I watch people "arise from the dust," change their lives, seal their families in the temple, and help others do the same, I marvel at God's great love for all of His children.

Think of the various cycles God has put into motion—hours and days, months and years, seasons and tides, planting and harvesting, birth and death, youth and age, and on and on. Think of the *power* and *pull* of orbiting planets and other celestial spheres in a rapidly expanding universe. Now think of the *power* and *pull* of celestial families! What a cycle! Maybe all those other cycles are but a shadow of the most important cycle of all—eternal families.

Think of that cycle—parents having children who grow and become parents who have children who grow, become parents, have children—eternal families being formed forever. Is that not the essence of eternal life? Is that not what we all innately seek? Is that not what the prophet Nephi alluded to? "For he that diligently seeketh shall find; and the mysteries of God shall be unfolded unto them, by the power of the Holy Ghost, . . . wherefore, the course of the Lord is *one eternal round*" (1 Nephi 10:19; emphasis added).

And just think, God has made it possible for all of us to be part of this eternal round of never-ending joy in our families! How could we not do everything in our power to achieve this joy?

When our family left Idaho Falls thirty years ago, we had a houseful of young children. Now only Jean and I were returning, but those same children are launching their own eternal families, and their children are on their way to doing the same. What a cycle! How good God is to all of us!

I know it is possible for everyone to eventually achieve the vision of an eternal family. We may have challenges in mortality that seem beyond our control, such as being sick or single or uncertain, but there is nothing in time or eternity that is beyond the Savior's ability to heal. As we yield our hearts to Him, He will help us get from where we are to where we need to be so we can obtain a fulness of joy. No one is beyond the reach of His love.

President Howard W. Hunter made this beautiful promise: "No blessing, including that of eternal marriage and an eternal family, will be denied to any worthy individual. While it may take somewhat longer—perhaps even beyond this mortal life for some to achieve this blessing, it will not be denied" (*Ensign*, June 1989, 75).

What a promise! It is made to any worthy individual—so we need to ask: How can we tell if we are worthy, or becoming so? Going to the temple is one key. If we have a deep desire to be in the temple, even if our present circumstances won't allow it, we are on the right path. If we feel comfortable when we are in the temple, we know we are on the right path. On the other hand, if we don't attend the temple or if we don't feel comfortable when we are there, we know we must change. It is vitally important to learn to feel at home in the temple, which is the Lord's house on earth. How can we expect to feel comfortable with Him in heaven if we don't feel comfortable with Him here?

Another key is to ask ourselves: Are my words and actions helping to set in motion that which will become part of God's eternal round? Every testimony borne, every blessing given, every calling fulfilled, every child brought righteously and unselfishly into this world and lifted into a cycle of righteousness—even every diaper changed, every meal prepared, every encouragement given, every smile projected, every example of patience set—is part of elevating ourselves and others into His eternal rounds of joy. The helpful things we do, which often bring no worldly recognition, in many ways are the most important. God's help and approbation will be with us in all our righteous efforts, no matter how mundane they may seem. How fulfilling to return to our heavenly home knowing we have helped move someone (including ourselves) into the Lord's orbit of eternal joy! The good we do, the sacrifices we make, the obedience we give, the unselfish help we render, and the inspired visions we faithfully follow live forever.

As Jean and I prepared to leave our home in Bountiful and return to Idaho Falls, I began to wonder about our definition of home. Bountiful had been the home base from which we left and to which we returned several times over many years. We had a deep and warm love for our ward members, neighbors, and other friends, and it was difficult to leave them. We have felt the same way each time we have moved to and from our various assignments. It is clear to me that home is wherever we have lived among people we have loved, speaking languages we have learned, and sharing teachings, testimonies, and experiences that have brought us closer to God and to each other.

Yes, home is wherever I can be with Jean and our family. Home is much more a "being together" than any particular physical location. We should sink our roots wherever we are planted, neither getting so deeply rooted that we refuse to leave or being so unrooted that we are anxious to leave. We should not get too tightly tied to anything of this earth, but rather get very tightly tied to each other, our family, and God!

We all have calls to serve, especially in our families, and we should do so with joy in our hearts. Everyone, everywhere, every time can be an instrument in God's hands to bring about His purposes, which purposes include our own eternal families and

Ready to go to the Idaho Falls Temple.

our own eternal joy. There is hope for all of us. We have not arrived yet, but as we acknowledge His hand and obey His plan, we will continue to participate in His eternal round, which is an opportunity to grow and develop forever. How I pray that none of us will spin ourselves out of that cycle through apathy, neglect, procrastination, or selfishness!

Anytime is a good time and anywhere is a good place to prepare to meet our Maker, but the best places on earth to do that are in our homes and in His holy temples. All of God's dealings with His children are to the end of creating eternal families, which is not an end at all but a beginning and a continuation of His work. This work becomes progressively deeper and broader and more fulfilling, and never ends (see Moses 1:37–39).

I hope that in every situation, wherever we are and whenever we are there, our actions will lift us and others into God's eternal round of joy anytime, anywhere—or, better stated, every time, everywhere!

TIME LINE		
1976–1978	Called to be a General Authority—April 3, 1976 Moved from Idaho Falls to Honolulu, Hawaii Area Supervisor for Hawaii—Pacific Islands Area	10 children
1978–1987	Moved to Bountiful, Utah Served in: Arizona/Nevada Northern California and Hawaii North Central United States Tonga, Samoa, Fiji, Tahiti Utah North Utah South North America West (California and Hawaii)	11 children 4 weddings
1987–1990	Lived in Buenos Aires, Argentina Served in South America South Area Presidency (Argentina, Chile, Uruguay, and Paraguay)	5 children 3 missionaries
1990–1994	Returned to Bountiful, Utah Served in North America West Area Presidency (California and Hawaii)	3 children at home 2 missionaries 3 weddings
1994–1998	Lived in Hong Kong Served in Asia Area Presidency (23 countries in Asia)	1 child at home 1 missionary 2 weddings
1998–2005	Returned to Bountiful, Utah Served in Utah North and Utah South Area Presidencies Called as one of the seven presidents of the Seventy—April 2004 Worked in the Idaho, Mexico, and Central America Areas	Empty nest
2005	Given emeritus General Authority status—Oct. 2005 Called to serve as president and matron of the Idaho Falls Temple—Nov. 2005	

INDEX